7 Steps to a Happier Family

First published in 2001 by
Marino Books
an imprint of Mercier Press
16 Hume Street Dublin 2
Tel: (01) 661 5299; Fax: (01) 661 8583
E-mail: books@marino.ie

Trade enquiries to CMD Distribution
55A Spruce Avenue
Stillorgan Industrial Park
Blackrock County Dublin
Tel: (01) 294 2560; Fax: (01) 294 2564
E.mail: cmd@columba.ie

© Kevin Flanagan and
Brian Mooney 2001

ISBN 1 86023 135 7

10 9 8 7 6 5 4 3 2 1

A CIP record for this title is available
from the British Library

Cover design by Penhouse Design
Cover illustrations and inside
illustrations by Cathy Dineen
Printed in Ireland by ColourBooks,
Baldoyle Industrial Estate, Dublin 13

7 Steps to a Happier Family

Kevin Flanagan and Brian Mooney

Dedications

I would like to dedicate this book to those who do not think they come from, or deserve to belong to, a happy family. For, like the perfect marriage, the perfect happy family is a rare thing. It is the striving to achieve happiness and harmony that matters. And finally may I dedicate this book to my own imperfect but sometimes happy family!

Kevin Flanagan

This book is dedicated to the memory of my late father, Edmund Mooney, 1922–99, and to my beloved wife Teresa.

Brian Mooney

Contents

1

The Myth of the Happy Family

And they all lived happily ever after, and now it is time to close your eyes, go to sleep and dream of happy things, before we must wake to the real world of pain and struggle. We all remember those wonderful days of childhood, when a mother's smile removed all worries and anxieties, when good always overcame evil and a never-ending horizon opened up before us, in which all uncertainty had been removed. In our adult world we crave the security provided by the stories we learnt in childhood. We relive them in stories and films, which open up for us a world of happy relationships that seems to be always beyond our grasp but is being enjoyed by most people around us. We curse our own misfortune that we are experiencing personal unhappiness, conflicting goals, frustrated relationships and a sense that we are not understood or loved for who we are. We believe that these experiences are uniquely ours and are not being experienced by those around us. We look around at all the seemingly happy people in our environment, be it the office, factory, sports club or neighborhood, and long for the happy lives those people appear to be living.

These seemingly happy people are the Jacks and Jills of this world, steadily climbing their hill. They seem to have the perfect life. He has already reached a good middle-management position, earns over £40,000 per year, drives a mid-range BMW and is rumoured to be in line for captain of the golf club next year. She, on the other hand, appears to be effortlessly combining her career as a barrister with her role as mother to three beautiful, healthy children. In recent years, with the children all in school, she has been able to work for a growing number of solicitors and is regarded by her peers as a good advocate in court. The children enjoy school and the reports from teachers on their progress have been positive, apart from the small matter of disruptive conduct on the part of the middle child, which the teacher puts down to attention-seeking. The eldest boy is quite a sports man and is playing for the school team. These people represent the fruits of our Celtic Tiger economy: they are the family we would all love to belong to.

Ah yes, but we are forgetting the nursery rhyme. It was not all plain sailing for Jack and Jill. Who are those people lining up to try and trip up poor Jack? The ambitious, late-twenties, information-technology graduates, who regard Jack as being no longer at the cutting edge and past his sell-by date? Or is it those in senior management who are studying the recently commissioned consultancy report on efficiencies, which recommends that a complete layer of middle management can be replaced with a series of new software packages? These are the same men and women who have supped at Jill's dinner parties and praised her for the quality of her entertainment. They are the people who have spoken about what an invaluable contribution Jack is making to the firm. Poor old Jack: he is working so hard to hold it all together and stay ahead of the pack, with all those bastards out to get him. Got to keep smiling; can't show them that he's not sleeping well and that at times everything seems to overwhelm him.

And what about poor Jill? What did the rhyme say: 'and she came tumbling after'? Sad to say, but behind her perfectly made-up face, as she glides from car to front door in view of the envious neighbors, lies a tormented woman. The balancing act of loving wife, adoring mother, watchful daughter and ambitious barrister is wearing her down. If only the damn jury had not spent five hours coming to such an obvious verdict, she would not have had to ring her aging mother yet again and ask her to collect the children from school, feed them and supervise their homework, so that she could collect them in the late evening, only to bring them home and put them straight to bed. Why is it that jurors all appear to have seen *Twelve Angry Men,* and act accordingly?

And what's wrong with Jack? she asks herself. He seems so preoccupied these days; he appears never to notice her any more, has not made love to her in months and flies off the handle whenever he is asked to help around the house, especially at weekends. He seems to see it as his God-given right to be in the golf club almost every Saturday. If she did the same, the house would fall down around them. But we could never have that, she thinks; not in this neighborhood.

What is going through the minds of James, Jane and Joe as they climb into their beds and Jane pleads with Jill to read them a story from her favorite book? They know that mum left them waiting at the school gate yet again, for ages. It was so embarrassing, in front of all their friends, and this was the fourth time it had happened this term. Dad had promised James that he would be there for his cup match last week, only to arrive ten minutes before the end of the game, embarrassing his son further by shouting out his praises every time the ball came within ten yards of him. Jane wants her mum to pay attention to the story and stop skipping lines in an effort to finish it. Why can't she read it like she used to? And it is so unfair of James to say that he wants to go to sleep when he is secretly listening to every word. Joe remembers the picture that he painted in class today, which got two stars from teacher and which he brought home to show his mum, but he instinctively knows that she would not want to look at it now. Maybe he will get a chance to show it to her in the morning.

Such are the joys of family life. Human beings growing in wisdom and understanding as the events that form our lives wash over us. Every member of our fictitious family imagines that life is so much more fulfilling in the homes of their friends and colleagues. How can we improve the quality of family life? In this book Kevin and I will ask you to look at seven aspects of your life. We will present you with various exercises within each area to help you explore issues that you might wish to work on.

But before we begin to explore our strengths and weaknesses, let us step back and try to undo some of the damage caused by the expectations raised in childhood by the line 'And they lived happily ever after.' What can we, be we men, women or children, hope to experience in family groups living as we do in a first-world economy at the beginning of the twenty-first century? If we are honest with ourselves and think about it for a little while, we will have no problem identifying our innermost needs. If we can be again in our minds the small children we all once were, and ask ourselves the question, what were the central issues in determining the quality of family life, we will have no problem in identifying them. The central issues were:

•   The certainty that in your family there was someone who was there for you whenever you needed love, understanding, support, encouragement, a shoulder to cry on or a word of praise that gave special meaning to an act or deed

- The awareness that home was a place where you experienced unconditional love and acceptance. It was a place where you could take off the mask that you presented to the outside world as you closed your front door, and you could become your unreconstructed, grumpy, self-centred self and still find acceptance

- The security of having a place to throw off your shoes, an arena where you can fight and argue, lose your temper and know that, by tomorrow, everything will be forgiven and forgotten

- The knowledge that in all the world there is one place where you can expect your needs to be met, be they food and shelter, or more profound ones of the soul or spirit, not because of what you can give in return but because of who you are

- The growing awareness that, at its core, home is a place where we make demands on others and they on us, and where the only currency is the love we have for each other

Family life is the central experience of the human condition. We are all drawn to be members of some family group, whatever its nature. The familiy group provides us with the basic building blocks of physical, emotional, psychological and spiritual well-being.

No matter what our experience of family life has been in the past, we continue to be drawn to set up or become members of families, while simultaneously resenting the shortcomings and limitations that a family places on us as individuals. We invariably feel that our efforts to create happiness within our families fall well short of what is achievable. This may be the motivating factor in leaving the home to establish a new family unit – we hope that, this time, we will get it right. The sad truth is that, in this search for the holy grail of family happiness, which is perceived to be attainable in a way that in the authors' opinion is purely imaginary, we leave in our wake brokenness, pain and a deep sense of loss. In this book we will attempt to explore the true potentiality of family life, its ultimate possibilities and its inevitable limitations. We will attempt to dispel the myth of 'happily ever after' and explore the true possibilities of human families.

2

Reflections on the Happier Family

The History of Family Life

Before we look at the reality of twenty-first-century family life, let us take a look back at the history of family life. Families as we experience them today are unique to our own time. They are radically different from the family of fifty years ago, and from human families as they existed for hundreds of thousands of years until the invention of agriculture and thus settled communities about 3,500 years ago. In large areas of today's world, families are about survival. The efforts of each and every member from dawn to dusk go into this collective struggle for survival. Success means ensuring that sufficient food is acquired by nightfall to feed every mouth. Beyond this is the luxury of putting hope in good fortune.

Prior to the establishment of agricultural settlements in around 1500 BC, humans' common experience was nomadic. Families consisted of large groups of adults and children, who with their animals moved from pasture to pasture in a constant struggle for survival. Even today in certain parts of the world this is still a daily experience, as nomadic groups lead their herds of animals over mountain valleys and across rivers in a never-ending struggle to repeat the timeless ritual of life.

It is interesting to look at the characteristics of such family groups, as it will help us to understand the genesis of the stresses and strains that families experience today. In nomadic cultures, everyone has a defined role, which never changes. From the moment of birth until death, ones destiny and actions are completely determined by the overriding demands of group survival, and every day is filled with urgent tasks with the aim of achieving this goal. There is no time for reflection on what might be, as circumstances determine all actions. When old age or sickness makes it impossible for the family group to get both a particular person and the animals across the next fast-flowing river, the animals come first because the survival of the family depends on their survival. Life in such communities is very simple. You are born and reared. You contribute to the collective effort to survive from the moment you are able and continue in your assigned role until you are no longer able to do so. You bear children to ensure the survival of the family, and when you become too great a burden on them, you move quietly away to die.

The development of agriculture and the growth of settled communities changed the nature of family life completely. The ownership of property brought with it the advent of class structures and all that flowed from that. Families were no longer large, interdependent groups but single units made up of grandparents, parents, unmarried brothers and sisters and children. Many of us old enough to have been living in Ireland prior to 1970 remember such families well. In many ways, they were not all that different from nomadic families, except that survival was not a day-to-day concern. Food was plentiful but basic and few went to bed hungry. Everybody had a roof over their head and a bed to sleep in.

But in other ways, a great deal had not changed. Food was grown on the land and in gardens near the house. Meat and poultry and their by-products, milk and eggs, were also provided from home. Money played a very small role in family life, being provided from the sale of animals or from a creamery cheque. It was used sparingly for the purchase of basic supplies such as tea, sugar, flour, shoes, clothing, and a few drinks in the pub for the men. As in nomadic cultures, roles were clearly defined. Everybody knew from an early age what life had in store for him or her. The eldest son would inherit the land or business. Daughters could hope to marry an eldest son and move on to a neighboring farm or business. Beyond that, there was the Church or nursing. Younger sons also had the option of the Church, the emigrant boat or, for the lucky few who stayed on at school beyond fourteen, a job in the bank or the civil service. On farms, depending on their size and the goodwill of the owner, younger brothers and sisters could choose to stay at home as unmarried helpers, receiving bed and board for the price of their labour. As in the past, the question of expectations did not arise for most people. They would live out their lives in roles that had remained unchanged for centuries.

If we contrast the nature of families as described above with the reality of family life as we experience it today, we will see that the stresses and strains that we are experiencing now are directly attributable to the unique, and completely new, nature of twenty-first- century families. In place of multi-generational family groups, most of our family units are made up of one generation of adults with children. The definition of what constitutes a family has also broadened considerably. There may be one or two parents living with children, couples living together without children, widowed people living alone or with their married or unmarried children, people living alone or sharing their lives with a much-loved pet, same-sex couples, friends living together on a long-term non-sexual basis, religious communities and so on. The main point to be made is that, in the modern family as described above, roles and expectations are open to continuous change and development. Let us now look at the changing roles of men and women in twenty-first-century family life.

Family Life in the Twenty-first Century

Man enters the twenty-first century with many question marks hanging over his identity and role. No longer can he assume that, on reaching adulthood, he will be regarded as the head of his household, the breadwinner, the decision-maker, the controller of the finances within the family, the undisputed boss. Given recent advances in medical technology, even his role in the fathering of children is no longer essential. Stripped of all the certainties which previously surrounded the role of men in the family, many teenagers today experience a growing sense of dis-orientation as they contemplate their futures. Because society does not give males the same opportunities to explore and express emotional issues as it does females, many more young men than women take their own lives.

As a teacher for twenty-five years and as a counsellor in recent years, I have worked with others in education to develop and present programmes that have attempted to deal with these issues. The introduction of relationship and sexuality programmes and recently created courses on masculinity have greatly assisted young men in reflecting on, and writing about, relationship issues. I am constantly seeing, on a one-to-one basis, students who raise privately with me issues that are dealt with in such classes. It is a very brave young man who will publicly talk about these matters in front of their peers, but I can state without fear of contradiction that they are more focused in such classes than in any other subject. I might be tempted to believe that the reason for such a level of interest on the part of students comes from the quality of my own work, and my relationship with them. The truth is much more likely to be that, within their own families, they experience the pain and suffering of observing the slow disintegration, and sometimes the death, of their parents' relationship. Now that it has become socially acceptable for married couples to separate in Ireland, we are seeing growing numbers of fathers living apart from their wives and children. Who or what is to blame for this situation?

As a child of the 1950s, I grew up in a society where the message to every young men was that his success or failure as a person would be measured by his career. At school, this message was reinforced on a daily basis. Despite the fact that paid work takes up on average a third of one's daily life, while sleep consumes another third, the question of what skills one required to navigate the other eight hours successfully was never raised. In recent years, a fellow past pupil showed me a photograph of our class. In the front desk sat two students, both of whom subsequently took their own lives. This made me realize how important it is for society to reflect very carefully on the messages we give our children, and how vital it is to ensure that our education system deals with the whole person. This involves all aspects of life: intellectual, physical, emotional, psychological, spiritual, social and interpersonal. It disturbs me to see parents taking their children out of mainstream schools where many of the above skills are integrated into educational programmes and placing them in grind schools where they can focus totally on academic work. I wonder whether they realize the possible long-term consequences of their actions for their children.

In dealing with fathers whose marriages have broken down, I have shared the intense pain of those whose professional lives are models of success and whose personal lives lie in pieces around them. When they are able to reflect honestly on the underlying problems that precipitated the eventual breakdown, most men admit that they lacked the language to express their emotions. In many cases, this lack of emotional capacity did not manifest itself in the early years of the relationship, when the effort to consolidate careers, acquire a home, give vent to ones hormonal drives and experience the joy of parenthood absorbed all the energies of both partners. For many of these relationships, the problems began to manifest themselves after the summit had been scaled and success in all ones initial goals had been achieved.

In my experience, these problem tend to manifest themselves gradually as both partners live out their roles they learnt in childhood. The gap between one partner's expectations and needs in terms of their emotional life and the other partner's capacity to reciprocate gradually draws the lifeblood from the relationship, until one day the realization dawns on one or both of them that the relationship is dead. The need today for both parties to a relationship to develop skills in emotional expression is heightened by the lifespan of the twenty-first-century adult. Never in human history have people lived together for so long without the distraction of the constant struggle for survival. With advances in modern medicine, this problem is going to get bigger, as we all live longer, healthier lives. Educators will have to continuously address the question as to whether our education system prepares people for the full range of skills that twenty-first-century life demands.

This seems to be a bigger challenge for men than it is for women. Sadly, proficiency at work and on the sports field is not sufficient to guarantee a happy family life. If you are a man reading this book and want to know whether you need to undertake some personal-development work, as dealt with in the previous chapters, answer the following question: what feeling do you experience as you turn the key in your front door as you return home at the end of the day? If the answer is 'joy and expectation', you can close this book right now. If, on the other hand, it is a certain tightness in the chest or a mild sense of apprehension, read on.

For women, the twenty-first century brings its own set of problems, which are very different from those of men. One of the greatest, if not *the* greatest, change in human history occurred in the 1960s with the invention of the contraceptive pill. This allowed women, for the first time in human history, to control their fertility, and therefore revolutionize their role in society. Women were no longer obliged to retire from work on getting married, as had been the case for people in public service in Ireland until the early 1970s.

Their lives no longer controlled by pregnancy and childbirth, women have continued to join the paid labour force in ever-increasing numbers. I remember going to work in London in 1972 and being amazed at the number of women who were in paid employment. Since then, changes in the nature of our economy have further facilitated this process. By this, I am referring to the growth in service industries to over 60 per cent of the economy. This trend facilitates growing female participation in the paid labour force, as the skills required in services are possessed by women in equal if not greater measure than by men.

This process has led to the two-income family becoming the norm in society today. It has also led to a situation where a family needs two incomes to have – and maintain – a decent standard of living today. This particularly applies if you wish to purchase your own home. The problem that this creates for women today is that they regard their partner as just that: a partner. They see their partner as someone who makes a 50 per cent contribution to every aspect of family life: financial, domestic, childcare, emotional-expression, and so on. As I have stated previously, men have no problem with enjoying the benefits of the second salary. On the other hand, some are still trying to get their minds around the implications of the other aspects of partnership – and I am not talking about the 1890 Partnership Act.

The second problem for women is that, for all the modernity of twenty-first-century living, life for the majority of women is still centred on their role as mothers of children. The modern woman has to fulfill her eternal role as bearer and rearer of children alongside her role as coequal partner in the twenty-first-century economy. The stresses and strains on women caused by these conflicting roles is a major contributory factor to the problems of family life today.

Given greater life expectancy, most of us will live into our seventies and eighties. This age group is the fastest-growing segment of the population. Many people today experience over twenty years of retirement. What hopes and expectations of family life do this group have? If both partners are still alive and living happily together, they deserve our praise and respect. For many elderly people, their main experience of family life is minding their grandchildren, to enable their daughter or daughter-in-law to pursue a career. Many elderly people find this work quite physically stressful but feel that it is impossible, given the circumstances, to raise any objections to it. They are also aware of the pain of loneliness and do not want to drive their children away from them. The problems of healthy living, into old age, are a welcome addition to the list of difficulties to be confronted in the twenty-first century, and one to which we as a society will have to pay far more attention in the future. Finally let us look at the changing role of children in our society.

The Changing Role of Children

When I was young, your status among your peers was measured by the size of your bag of marbles and your ability – or lack of it – to kick a ball around a football pitch. Working as I am today as a counsellor to young people, I have a window into a world where the demands on them to grow up faster than they or their parents might wish is overwhelming. The source of this pressure is our modern economy. Parents, who are wealthier than any previous generation, have transferred huge spending power to their children, who have thus become the object of marketing and advertising by business and industry. This leads to enormous peer pressure from within the young person's age group to have the full range of 'must have' possessions. This process has also driven children to take up part-time jobs to finance the lifestyle to which they believe they have a right. Part of this lifestyle may be experimentation with drugs and alcohol, as well as an expectation of sexual activity at an earlier age than for previous generations. Again, we as a society will have to give a great deal of thought as to how to protect our children from the stresses and strains of adult life until they are mature enough to handle them. Allowing them to holiday together in the Canaries at sixteen and seventeen years of age may not be the wisest way to start.

Having looked at the changing nature of what we perceive families to be and at the changing roles and expectations of males and females of all age groups within such families, we must now address the main reason for writing this book. Whether you are the child, the parent, the partner, the grandparent, the uncle or the aunt, you must ask yourself, what you can do in your life today to make living in your family easier and happier for both yourself and those around you. Remember the golden rule: you can never change anyone except yourself. Others change in response to the changes you make in yourself. Kevin and I will now examine seven different aspects of your life that you may be able to make positive changes in. As a result of your work on yourself – and remember, meaningful change is slow and gradual and takes time to show results – you will hopefully experience a growth in harmony and cooperation in your family life.

The Reality of Irish Family Life Today

My experience of the Irish family starts with my experience of my own family in childhood. As I grew up, I came to know my wider family, my neighbors and the families of my friends. On getting married, I discovered a whole new family, which was far larger than my own. On becoming a counsellor, I entered the lives of hundreds of families. Through all these years, I have learned some truths, which I will now share with you.

The third chapter of the Book of Genesis tells us the story of the nature of the relationship between man and woman outside the Garden of Eden. She will experience pain in childbirth and be ruled over by her husband. He will have a life of sweat and toil. Their two sons will fall out with each other and one will kill the other. As it started at the beginning of human history, so it continues today.

Anyone who would tend to idealize the family of the past need only read the writings of Frank McCourt about his life growing up in Limerick, or the plays of Sean O'Casey, which deal with life in Dublin in the early part of the twentieth century. Recent television documentaries on the plight of children raised in so-called care in various institutions under the supervision of the state, and of young women who became pregnant outside marriage and experienced the total rejection of the father of their child, their own family, and the society they lived in, show us that life in Irish families was never far from the picture painted in Genesis. Even in recent years, the courts have brought forward the most horrific cases of sexual and physical abuse occurring within families. One of my earliest cases as a counsellor related to a young woman who had been sexually abused for years within her own family.

Hopefully your experience of family life is not, and has not been, as painful as those described above. All of us, myself included, can look back at our experience of family life and see its strengths and weaknesses. We can remember days when we wished we were members of some other family and other days when we felt very lucky. Suffice to say that families are our bedrock, our point of reference.

Without them, we would be crushed by an overwhelming sense of disorientation, lack of identity and disconnectedness.

We need go no further than the situation of the adopted child in a secure, loving home who is still driven to discover her original birth parents. Sometimes this search can bring great happiness. On other occasions, it can lead to great pain.

Marian was adopted at birth and grew up in a loving home. She never experienced any need to find out who her birth parents were until she was about to get married. She asked her adoptive parents to assist her in discovering her natural parents. After some initial difficulties, she eventually located them in Belfast. Her mother had given her up for adoption when she was sixteen but had subsequentially married Marian's father. They now had ten children. Marian had gone to very good schools and had received a university education. Her ten brothers and sisters had grown up in a very different environment. Having discovered their whereabouts, and brought them into her life, what choice had she but to invite them to her wedding?

The day started well enough – that is, until they arrived at the hotel. As often happens in these situations, the meal was delayed for nearly two hours, by which stage her natural family was in great form, having consumed large quantities of drink. The trouble really started when her natural father took it upon himself to contest with her adoptive father the right to give the father-of-the-bride speech. After Marian's father had eventually been persuaded to sit down, the speeches were given in a state of some tension as a string of bawdy one-liners emanated from the direction of the table of her natural family. By this stage, sections of her husband's family were beginning to see their very recently acquired member in a new light and were beginning to wonder whether a dreadful mistake had not just occurred. Marian had always wondered about her past; now she knew.

The Struggle for Power

All our families are the by-product of humans' need for meaningful relationships. They are also in most cases a by-product of the natural expression of our sexuality. We need them but are engaged in a constant struggle for power within them. Newborn babies learn very quickly how to exert power within their family. The only requirement for this is a healthy pair of lungs. As they grow, they may find that a smile works wonders in getting the desired amount of attention. And so the learning process, which starts at birth, continues until we draw our last breath.

This struggle for power underlies many difficulties that I deal with in my work as a counsellor. These difficulties can arise out of the struggle between two adults, who may be partners, or between a person and a parent, or possibly between a wife or husband and their mother- or father-in-law. In this final chapter, I will examine some of the causes of conflict between various parties within families and look at various insights I have gained over the years regarding how to resolve such conflicts.

The struggle for power between two partners is the unspoken reality of all family groups. It may revolve around seemingly simple things, such as how one should leave the bathroom after one has finished with it, to major power issues such as whether to try for a child now or to postpone such a plan in order to enable both parties to develop their careers. The vast range of mother-in-law stories points to the struggles that often occur between mothers and their sons- or daughters-in-law. These struggles form the backdrop to the daily experience of family life that most of us live with. Such struggles are perfectly healthy and can lead to rows and arguments, which are resolved by discussion and compromise on both sides.

When one party attempts to impose their position on all other parties, however, the relationship of mutual respect that human beings should hold for each other breaks down and is replaced by the exercise of power and control as a means of resolving conflict within the family. The controlled party or parties can either enter into an ongoing state of sullen resistance, defying the controller at every available opportunity, can choose to break up the family or leave it, or can accept the nature of the relationship and suffer a gradual loss of self-respect and personal self-worth, becoming a shadow of their potential self. If you recognize yourself in any of the above roles, I would suggest that you begin the attempt to bring about change in your life. Change is always painful and you are the only one who can make it.

If you are the controller – the bully – ask yourself, what is the real quality of the relationship between you and those you bully? You will only get to live one life and the quality of your relationships determines the quality of your experiences. Can you truly say that you are happy? When you look at those in your family, can you not see the untapped potential within each one of them: their ability to grow and develop as persons, and enrich both their own life and yours ?

If you are the victim of such a parent or partner, you must realize that, as we have stated many times in this book, the only person you can change in this life is yourself. To make changes in situations and patterns of behavior that have existed for years may seem like an in-surmountable task. You will probably need the help and assistance of a listening ear, be it of a friend, another family member or a professional counsellor. You must realize that all of us are capable of change, if we can perceive the benefit of such changes. By slowly bringing about changes in your own behaviour patterns and in how you respond to various situations, you confront others with the new reality of your self, thus opening up for them a transformed reality to which they must respond.

If you calmly explain that you are no longer prepared to repeat the pattern of the relationship of the past and that you are making changes in your own life which you are not prepared to reverse, and then invite them to build a better quality of relationship based on mutual respect, you may be surprised by the positive response you receive. If, having attempted this process for a period of time, you meet with an ongoing negative response, it would be our advice that you consider leaving the relationship. Painful as this leap into the unknown may be, if we relinquish our sense of personal dignity and self-respect we have given up the essential ingredient of what it means to be human. This is too high a price to pay for any relationship.

The option to separate – to break up or leave a relationship – is one that has been exercised by a growing number of people in recent years. Some would see this as a consequence of our consumerist society, where advertisers implant within us from an early age an expectation of instant gratification of our wants. They would state that this consumerist outlook leads us to see a relationship as something to be experienced, as opposed to something we create and build. There is much truth in this perception. Successful relationships are the result of very hard work and an attitude of self-sacrifice and long-term commitment, as we have seen from the seven-step process. They are not products to be enjoyed in the short term and traded in for the next model as we become bored with the first.

Having stated this, it may also be the case that terminating a relationship may be in the best interests of all involved. One has only to witness the long-term effects on both adults and children of living in a family where any attempt to build quality relationships has long been abandoned. In these environments, a war of attrition takes over, in which everybody and every issue become a potential weapon in the struggle between partners.

I am amazed in my work at the amount of pain and suffering that partners are prepared to inflict on each other and on their children as a by-product of the battles they wage. I see many children with tears running down their faces as they describe in faltering voices the reality of their homes. They talk about the continuous fights that are sparked by the most trivial of incidents, about the shouting matches in which nobody listens to what anyone else is trying to communicate, and about homes in which no meals get prepared and everybody learns to survive by getting through each day on their nerves. They also describe the humiliation of never being able to bring friends around to play, out of fear of what might erupt at any moment.

I am amazed that many of these children become so conditioned to seeing this reality as being normal that they continually resist the idea of their parents separating. In their imaginations, they create fantasy worlds in which their parents overcome their difficulties and happy family life is created. These fantasies are perpetuated even though the day-to-day reality has been a living hell for years. I often deal with children who are manifesting severe behavioral problems brought about by their parents' decision to separate, even though they have lived with deep unhappiness and conflict for years. They must at last face the reality of what, by fantasizing, they have been avoiding for years.

Over time, these children come to accept the new situation and see that the new reality of their family's circumstances allows everyone involved to rebuild their lives and possibly recover their sense of personal dignity. If you recognize yourself as an adult party in the type of family that I have described here, I would advise you to consider the long-term damage you are inflicting on yourself, your partner and your children. What lessons are they learning about how to develop and build relationships? Have you the right, by failing to deal constructively with the reality of your situation, to cripple the capacity of all of your family members to build healthy relationships in the future? Moving on from the struggle for power between adults within families, let us now explore the relationship between adults and their children.

The Adult-Child Relationship

The teenage years are a time when young people begin to explore the limits of their power within the family. This exploration may take the form of sleeping in a room which appears to resemble a refuse tip but which is just perfect in their eyes. It can also involve very unusual hairstyles and clothing. It may even entail the piercing of various body parts. It also finds expression in demands for greater freedom to engage in activities that 'everybody else's parents' allow *their* children to engage in: going to discos, staying overnight with friends, going on holiday with groups of friends and so on.

Having worked with them for over a quarter of a century, I feel that I can speak with some authority on the subject of the modern Irish teenager. The first thing that parents need to realize is that it is in the nature of all young people to test the limits of their freedoms. What many parents seem not to realize is that asking is not the same as wanting. Just as important for young people is an awareness of where the boundaries to their push for freedom lie. All of us enjoy a sense of security from knowing and under-standing where the boundaries for behaviour exist in society. We know what to expect when we sit down beside someone in a public bus. They may ignore us, smile, engage in conversation and so on. They are not likely to sit on our lap and kiss us on the mouth. This awareness of unwritten rules gives us the freedom to travel freely on public transport.

Our children enjoy the same rights. They need to know where the boundaries of behaviour are, and to enjoy the security that this knowledge brings. Many parents think they are being very progressive in giving their children the freedom they demand. My work has shown me that children from such families are the unhappiest and most insecure. They keep looking for the security of knowing where the boundaries of their world are, and they cannot find them.

As a very young teacher, I was one of eight members of staff on a boat-and-coach tour of northern Europe with two coachloads of students. The teacher organizing the tour did not believe in exercising strict discipline over the students, as they were on holidays. Some senior students were found to have taken alcohol on the initial boat trip to England. Nothing was done about the incident. More students did the same thing on an overnight boat trip from England to Holland; again, nothing was done to stop it. A day or so later, a number of fourteen-year-old students were discovered, the worse for wear, having taken alcohol in Germany.

At this stage, an older member of staff stepped in and suggested that he speak to the entire student group. The following morning he boarded each coach prior to departure and outlined a list of rules to be observed for the remainder of the trip. On each bus, the students applauded him after he finished speaking. The atmosphere improved markedly from that moment on, and the rest of the trip passed without further problems. The students tested the limits of their freedom on day one, and found that there were no limits. Rather than react with joy at this discovery, their reaction was one of confusion and insecurity. Once boundaries had been laid down, everybody could get on with enjoying their tour.

What is the moral of this story for parents? Believe it or not, young people like rules, so long as they feel that they have been listened to, have been treated with respect and have had the reasons behind the decisions explained. They may continue to argue their case, and with the passing of time it may be appropriate to give them a greater degree of freedom. From my experiences of working with young people today, it seems to me that many parents are reacting against what they perceive as the too-authoritarian parenting of their own mothers and fathers by giving their own children total freedom. They are mystified as to why this has resulted in confused and rudderless children who do not seem to be very secure. In fact, good parenting involves knowing how to expand the boundaries of freedom in a gradual way and engaging in a real dialogue with the child, thus showing them that your boundaries are being set out of love and care and not out of the simple exercise of parental power.

In some families, the opposite is the case, with parents rigidly controlling their children's lives, making all the decisions for them. John was a fifth-year student who had selected his subjects for the Leaving Certificate. He came to see me to ask to change some of them. He told me that he was not enjoying a number of subjects and was doing poorly in them. He was also unsure of the reasons for his new choices. I refused to approve any changes until he could give me a rational reason for his choice. I next received a call from one of his parents asking to see me about the problem. Some days later, I sat across a desk from John, with his parents on either side of him.

It became clear very quickly that both parents had very different views of John's future. His father was certain that he wanted him to become an engineer; his mother was equally certain that she wanted him to become a solicitor. Neither would give an inch and they argued back and forth about it for some time. While this was going on, John was visibly shrinking further into his seat as they fought over his future. As tempers flared, I interjected with a comment: 'Maybe we should hear from John as to what he might see himself doing in the future?' His father said, 'What has this got to do with him?'

At this point, I asked everybody to reflect on what had just happened. John's future was being fought over by his parents as if he were a possession. They both had a vision of his future, and that was all that mattered. He was stuck in the middle, trying to keep both his parents happy, and was totally miserable. They were utterly blind to the fact that, as children grow, it is in the parents' best interests to allow them to take more and more decisions for themselves. This leads to a greater sense of personal responsibility on the children's part. Such steps are all part of the process of parents 'letting go' of their children; this process should start at a very early age.

Children should be presented with decisions as early as possible, and parents should ensure that they experience the consequences of their decisions. For example, if a young child has an allowance and asks to spend it in a particular way, his parents should point out that, whatever the money is spent on, the next allowance is a week away. They should then stick with that decision, no matter how much the child might plead with them for more money. This teaches children that decisions have consequences and that we must live with them. As the child grows up, the parents should ensure that their children take ever more important decisions. By this process, when the child enters their teenage years, they will know that they will have to accept the consequences of their actions.

You may ask whether I am contradicting what I said earlier regarding boundaries. I am not: my philosophy of child-rearing is that parents should have the courage to define boundaries for their children within which they can grow in safety. These boundaries should expand as the child grows. Within the boundaries, the child should be encouraged to reflect on and decide upon as many issues as possible.

The nature of the relationship between parents and their children in Ireland today can best be summed up by the reality of what takes place after Leaving Certificate results are issued each year. Many students head to the sun in groups, leaving parents to negotiate their way through the consequences of their child's points' score. In my counselling work, I have dealt with the consequences of that week in the sun. Isolated from their families and under huge peer pressure, many young people act in a way which they deeply regret later but cannot undo. Nor will they ever have the courage to tell their parents what transpired. In certain cases, this has led to the death of students, and deep trauma for their friends. Many of them are simply too young to handle decisions relating to alcohol, drugs and sex over a prolonged period, thousands of miles from their families, without the usual excuses that they would have at home if they wanted to back out without losing face in front of their peers. In my opinion, parents should have the courage to explain to their children that important decisions have to be taken regarding the students' careers, and that the students themselves should be there to make those decisions. They should further explain that what is fashionable may not always be right and that glossy brochures do not tell the full story of what can happen on holiday.

Other Challenges

One of the greatest changes to have affected family life in my lifetime is the growth of the media, especially television. I remember how much excitement there was when a neighbour rented the first television on our street. The neighbour's children suddenly acquired many additional friends. I also remember how games of chasing or marbles were suspended for the duration of *Lassie* or *The Fugitive.* The power of the media has grown enormously over the intervening years, and its effect on each member of the family is enormous, yet insidious. From early childhood it is forming our values and attitudes to life.

Soap operas aimed at teenagers create, over a number of years, real-life carbon copies of their characters. Having spent long periods in California over the last fifteen years, I have been deeply saddened to see young children, each one unique and different, reduced to clones of a media-created stereotype. Conversation is reduced to an imitation of the mindless babble of the afternoon soaps, with images of what constitutes worth or beauty being in the hands of highly skilled marketing departments. This has gone beyond the stage of control of dress and possessions and has reached the point where a whole generation has come to accept that our bodies need extensive plastic surgery before we can be successful in life. There is nothing so sad as seeing, at a social gathering, a middle-aged woman who has had all of the implants, nips and tucks available, monitoring, with anxiety in her eyes, who her partner is talking to.

Are we in danger of allowing the media to dictate the qualities that we value in human relationships? I believe that the advent of media studies within the school curriculum has heightened to some degree our awareness of the power of all forms of media in our lives. I further believe that every member of the family would benefit from discussions on why certain programmes are presented as they are. I believe that we can protect our values and beliefs by openly discussing the nature of what the media present to us, rather than always just passively sitting there looking at it.

We must of course remember that the nature of the family has changed in recent years. No longer can we presume that two parents living with their own offspring is the norm in society. The social stigma that drove thousands of girls into the Magdalene laundries in earlier years is thankfully gone. These women, if they decide to have their baby, are increasingly deciding to raise the child themselves. Over 30 per cent of children born in Ireland today live in such families. Sometimes these women marry; others form non-marital relationships that last various periods of time. It is quite normal today to be dealing in schools with children whose brothers and sisters are the offspring of a number of different fathers, one of whom may be living in the family home. These mothers have exercised their rights to fulfil their sexual needs in a way that would not have been possible even twenty years ago. In working with such children, I have found that they form a disproportionately large group of those who require the assistance of counselling. Their specific problems emanate from the circumstances of their homes.

Most unmarried mothers have to work – many of them in jobs with unsocial hours. This results in their children having less parental supervision than other children. They may also lack any male role model; this can have the effect of giving the message that man's only role in a child's life is to facilitate conception and move on. If the child takes on board this unspoken message, it is probable that this pattern will become established in perpetuity. Children growing up in such families may be at a disadvantage compared with other children. Apart from lacking a male role model, they are on average materially less well off than their peers. This may limit their access to educational resources and lead them to fail to achieve their potential. They may also not have an environment in which study is easily undertaken. Sometimes in working with such children one is caught between the reality of their lives and the expectations of their teachers.

Paul's family consisted of his mum, Barbara, who was in her mid-thirties, his sister Rachael, who was fifteen and was expecting a baby, and his younger sisters Jane and Margaret. His dad, Peter, who was married to his mum but was not Rachael's father, had left the family home and was now living forty miles away, with Angela, who has a baby boy, Andrew, and is also pregnant. Paul is getting into trouble in school because he is regularly missing homework and does not have the correct books. Sometimes he goes to his father for the weekend and, as his books are at home, no homework gets done. At home, things can get a bit lively at times between his mother and Rachael, who is off school as she is in the final months of her pregnancy. Paul's grandmother, who is in her early fifties and lives across the street from them, has promised to mind Rachael's baby so that she can return to school to complete her Junior Certificate.

Paul's parents are managing their lives well. They are taking responsibility for their children and dealing with life's events as they arise, in a loving and caring manner. The problems for this family arise as a result of their interactions with middle-class institutions like schools that have standards and expectations that are totally different from those of Paul's family. All society can do for the Pauls of this world is to provide additional resources in schools in the form of counselling and supervised study time after class, to ensure that he stays in school and completes his education. Within relationship and sexuality education, one would hope that he would come to see that long-term relationships are not only an option but a goal to be sought after, in that it provides the ideal environment for the growth and development for men, women and children.

Up to now, I have focused on adults and children in all kinds of circumstances in families in Ireland today – and on the relationships between adults and children. I have reflected on my own experiences of working with children for twenty-five years and have come to the conclusion that happy families are places in which adults spend time listening to their children and discussing with them the events of their day, even when, in their teenage years, the children tend to answer in a very uncommunicative manner. The point is to keep the lines of communication open and to send the message that you are always there for them and will not judge them, no matter what the circumstances.

How many young people have got into serious difficulties because they did not feel able to tell their parents their dilemma? I once found myself in the position of talking a young woman out of her decision to go to England to have an abortion – a decision she had taken because she did not believe her elderly widowed father would be able to cope with the news that she was having a baby. I organized for her to visit her sister in Canada, supposedly to work for a year, and have the baby there. The relief she expressed when she saw another way out other than abortion taught me the importance of keeping lines of communication between parents and children open.

The single biggest issue that degrades and eventually destroys the lines of communication between family members is substance abuse. It would be easy for me simply to say that people should know better. I have shared the pain of too many clients whose family lives have been destroyed by alcohol. I have watched with a growing sense of helplessness as the so-called recreational-drug culture has put down deep roots among young people. We need not be surprised that our young people look at the extent to which adult social and sporting life rotates around alcohol and choose to imitate this lifestyle, adding the extra element of drugs. One of the effects of our recent prosperity has been to give young people sufficient spending power to finance the consumption of large quantities of both alcohol and drugs almost every weekend. The addictive nature of such substances, be they cigarettes, drink or drugs, reduces the capacity of anyone who consumes them to be a positive influence on family life.

I have listened in silence to Gerry, a father of four, as he described his wife's slow disintegration into alcoholism. He outlined his frantic efforts to protect her, by searching the house on a daily basis to discover her hidden bottles of booze. He further described the total reversal of roles that took place, as his children instinctively compensated for their mother by taking responsibility for keeping life going on a day-to-day basis. As the words flowed, the inevitable final confrontation was described in painful detail: the detoxification process, the false dawns, and the support of Alcoholics Anonymous. I have heard this story repeated in many forms. I have seen broken-hearted parents bury their daughter, who committed suicide in a haze of alcohol-induced despair, with her friends huddled together in groups, numb with shock. I listen, in my work, to young people describe a typical weekend, telling how their pocket money – plus the income from their part-time jobs – is blown on alcohol and drugs. This is the Ireland of today.

I wonder whether it is futile to hope that these young people will not develop, in adulthood, a lifestyle built around dependence on such substances. Is it futile to believe it possible to protect oneself and ones family against this cancer, which is eating away at the soul of family life? Firstly, one must accept that alcoholism is a disease, which slowly seduces its victims. Secondly, we must realize that certain personalities have addictive characteristics that make them susceptible to such substances. Having said all this, I believe that it is possible to protect oneself and ones family.

Why do people drink alcohol? Why do young people take drugs at weekends? The simple answer is that they make people feel better, make them lose their inhibitions and give them a false sense of confidence. These attributes are available to all of us through the process of mutual support and encouragement. We all need to be attended to, to be affirmed, to be encouraged to develop our interpersonal and communication skills. It is only through this process of real growth that we will develop within ourselves and facilitate among our fellow family members the solid foundations of personal self-belief, which will make the taking of abusive substances seem unnecessary and destructive from the outset. This process requires hard work and a sense of personal honesty that calls for real courage. It is the hard road to human happiness, which requires years of patient love and care from those closest to us. It is the path we must take if we are to create the environment for a happy family life.

Happy families are also places in which adults are not fearful to set reasonable boundaries for their children – never forgetting to expand them as their children develop the capacity to handle more responsibility. Parents continuously complain to me that their children will not act responsibly, while the parents continue to accept all responsibility for them. At this point, I would like to give a word of advice to all those stressed mothers who ring me after the Leaving Certificate results wanting to know what little Johnnie should do now. Tell your children that you understand that they have some hard choices to make, that you are there for them and that you will facilitate any reasonable decision they come to, and then let them get on with figuring our their future.

Final thoughts

Happy families are places in which busy parents understand that it is not sufficient to give your children every material possession that they ask for, as compensation for the parents' presence from their lives. When you get your new diary in January, schedule periods each week when you will be with your children in an unstressed environment. This may seem like a strange idea, but diaries are meant to guide us through the important events of our year. What is more important than the time your children know you are there for them?

Finally, happy families are places in which adults have a healthy relationship with each other. They respect each other and accept that both parties have a sacred right to grow and develop to their full potential, and that each must accommodate this growth process. In the previous seven chapters, we looked at the needs that we all have as human beings. We examined ways in which you can improve the quality of each of those seven areas of your life. In applying the suggestions in your own life, you will inevitably improve the quality of your relationships. If you make changes in the way you yourself live, those around you, and especially members of your immediate family, will have to respond to those changes. If you do not attempt to ram down their throat the fact that you have made changes, they are probably going to enquire as to what motivated you to do so. This is the moment when you tell them about *7 Steps to a Happier Family.* Good luck in looking at your own needs and addressing them. We hope that the changes you make improve your contribution to family life and thus allow your family, if not to live happily ever after, then to continue to work towards the daily goal of greater harmony, self-respect and respect for others that constitute happy family life.

3

The Seven-Step Guide to a Happier Family

This seven-step guide is not a quick fix, instant cure or guarantee of success for having a happy family. Rather, it is part of the continuing process of maintaining that state. By 'process', we mean continuous and ongoing work on the relationship. In other words, the work is never finished.

'Process' v. 'Completed Package'

Modern psychology puts a lot of emphasis on 'process', and it is a useful concept. A lot of the time we are brought up to think that things are set in stone and permanent. We fall in love and assume that, once we discover this state of love, things will remain the same forever. But as those who have fallen in love know, it is not a permanent state. If you start to ignore your loved one or give your attention to another, the love will wither and die. You can fall out of love just as easily as you can fall in love! It is the same with creating a happy family. It will need continuous work, like servicing your car to keep it roadworthy. You won't just *find* a happy family – you will have to build one and maintain it. That is the process involved in having a happy family.

The first step in creating a happy family is to work on yourself first.

Work on Yourself First

They say in therapy that the only person you can change is yourself (and even that is hard to do!). If you are in a difficult family relationship, the only person you can guarantee changing is yourself – the others may see nothing wrong with themselves and may not want to change at all!

Change yourself and others will change

But it often happens that, when you start working on yourself and making changes in your own life, those around you change as well. The reasons for this are simple. People generally *react* to a certain pattern of behaviour. If you are in the habit of coming home, slumping down on the sofa and asking where your dinner is, your partner may be in the habit of reacting negatively. They may react with aggression: 'Get your own meal!' or 'Am I your slave?' or they may say nothing and secretly boil with resentment (which will erupt later over something trivial).

Now, it may be impossible to change your partner's reaction, as he or she may feel that your behaviour is unbearable, but you can, with effort and discipline, change your own behaviour. For example, you may go to the trouble of shopping and bring in a TV dinner that you can microwave. So instead of demanding to be fed, you proceed to feed both yourself and your partner.

Now what will such a change do to the attitude of your partner? Will they berate you for being selfish? No, they will sit down and enjoy the meal with you. If this behaviour continues, and you continue to bring home food and prepare it yourself, their behaviour will change permanently!

This is a scenario that many couples will immediately recognise. Just replace preparing a meal for any one of a thousand other jobs, like putting out the rubbish, taking out the kids or getting the shopping. It is the tiny, mundane, domestic tasks that cause most of the conflict in family situations, and if you want a happy family, it is these sorts of issues that will need to be addressed. But as our example shows, the one way to change your partner's attitude towards you is to change your own attitude first.

The following are the seven steps needed to be happier in yourself and to have a happier family. Each step is accompanied by a questionnaire, which will show you how you are doing. Try filling in the questionnaire several days or weeks later, and see if changes are being made. One final point: good luck with your journey!

Remember: habits form our behaviour. If you have bad habits, you will strengthen and ingrain them every time you practise them. If you have good habits they will be strengthened every time you do them. We also pass our habits on to our children and affect our partners and friends in life. The following seven steps will help you develop good and positive habits in your personal life and your family life.

Step 1
Having a Healthy Body

It is difficult to be a member of a happy family if you are not healthy. If you are sick, you will not enjoy family life and will become a burden on your family. For example, if you smoke yourself to death or shorten your life through stress or worry, you will not be around to enjoy your family life – even if it is blissfully happy!

Remember, smokers shorten their life by up to sixteen years. If you lead an unhealthy lifestyle, you cannot be happy in the true sense of the word (though alcoholics and drug users may convince themselves otherwise!). The first prerequisite of a happy family is a healthy family! Now, start with yourself. Just how healthy are you?

Questionnaire: How Healthy Am I?

In the chart opposite, give yourself 10 for each 'Yes' and 0 for each 'No', or award yourself a score somewhere in between. Add your score up, and then join up the lines on the chart to see at a glance how healthy you are.

	Healthy									Unhealthy
	10	9	8	7	6	5	4	3	2	1	0

Do I exercise daily? (0 for 'Yes')

Do I eat five servings of fruit and
vegetables daily?

Do I take time out to relax every day?

Do I deal with stress effectively?

Do I get regular, quality sleep?

Am I the right weight for my age?

Do I see a GP and go to the dentist
when I need to?

Are my blood pressure and cholesterol
levels healthy?

Do I smoke? (0 for 'Yes')

Do I ever take more than two alcoholic
drinks a day? (10 for 'No')

Now join up the dots to see a graph of your physical health.
Then add up your score and place it in one of the following
categories:

100–80 Congratulations – you are really looking after your
body!

79–70 Good – but a few improvements could be made

69–60 OK – but improvements in your lifestyle are
definitely needed

59–50 Borderline – you run the risk of undermining your
health

49–30 Poor – you are putting your health at definite risk

0–29 Warning – you are in grave danger of serious ill-
health. See your GP immediately!

Now let's look at the areas we have just examined:

Do I exercise daily? (10 for 'Yes')

Fill in your score here: ☐

Now describe your exercise routine in the space below:

What is the minimum amount of exercise I need to be healthy?

The American College of Sports Medicine, the 'oracle' for health practitioners, used to say that we needed to walk for at least thirty minutes daily to be healthy. Now they have changed this prescription, making a healthy lifestyle even more attainable. They now recommend that you 'keep active doing whatever you enjoy doing'.

By this they mean:

- Regular gardening
- Regular pleasure walks
- Regular golf
- Playing soccer with the kids
- Taking up a hobby that involves exercise, e.g. tennis, swimming, golf, hill-climbing

The key to all this is *activity* rather than sitting around all day. In fact, Ireland is turning into a nation of couch potatoes:

49

- 9 out of 10 Irish women don't exercise regularly
- 8 out of 10 Irish men don't exercise regularly

Ireland is becoming a nation of fatties and, as a consequence, has one of the highest levels of stroke and heart disease in the world.

Question: What does the average citizen of the state weigh in 2000 compared to 1990?

- The same?
- Four pounds more?
- Four pounds less?
- One stone more?
- One stone less?

Answer: The average person now weighs one stone more in 2000 compared to 1990!

This is a frightening fact! It would not be so frightening if the extra stone was made up of muscle. Unfortunately, it is made up of fat! The consequences of this are profound. This extra fat strains the heart, clogs up the arteries, increases the risk of heart disease and stroke and destroys self-esteem.

Question: Is it worth it?
Answer: No!
Solution: healthy eating and exercise.

Healthy Eating

Rather than try to go on yet another diet, let's look at a simple way to improve your eating habits. Follow these straightforward steps and you will vastly improve both your eating habits and your weight.

How Important are relationships to You?

- Eat at least five servings of fresh fruit or vegetables daily
- Cut down on sugar and sugary snacks. Have one a day as a treat and replace them with fruit
- Take the salt cellar off the table. Do not add salt. It will be painful for a week and then you won't miss it – and your blood pressure will fall
- Cut down on dairy produce: milk, eggs, cream and cheese. These foods raise cholesterol and lead to all sorts of allergies. Replace with olive oil (which you can pour on bread), and low-fat products
- Cut down on saturated fats, red meat, factory-produced chickens, farmed salmon and trout. Fresh sea fish and organic, free-range products are better
- Cut down on all meat consumption. Vegetarians who have a balanced diet are healthy and well. Replace meat with lentils, beans and pulses
- Increase pasta consumption and use of olive oil. Learn how to cook Mediterranean-style – people who live in that region have less heart disease
- Cut alcohol to two units daily, preferably red wine. This regime will lower your cholesterol and reduce your stress!

Question: What sort of activity do I need?
Answer: Anything that keeps your interest and elevates your heart rate.

Activities that Keep Your Interest

Remember, we are far more likely to do things that we love doing. We will get up early and do them very well! Now, the word 'enthusiasm' means 'being filled with God'; when we are enthusiastic, we are literally filled with 'God'-ness.

No wonder enthusiastic people do things well! So take a few minutes to decide what you really like doing in terms of activities and jot it down in the space below. It must be an activity that you enjoy doing! After you've jotted it down, take time to reflect and write below the activity where you can do it, on what days and for how long. Writing down the time, place and duration of any activity means you have had to think it through and as a result are more likely to complete it.

Now Let's Look at Some Activities You Can Do

- Gardening
- Walking
- Swimming
- Hill-climbing
- Orienteering
- Cycling
- Walking to work or the shops regularly instead of taking the car
- Tennis
- Golf
- Soccer
- Jogging
- Playing with the kids
- Taking up dance classes, e.g. salsa, tango, funk
- Taking up yoga or tae kwon do
- Getting a dog and walking it!

Of course, joining a gym and starting a proper exercise programme will ensure that you become comprehensively fit. A good fitness programme will ensure that you work on the five components of fitness. These are:

- Strength
- Flexibility
- Local muscular endurance
- Aerobic capacity
- Body-fat composition

Remember, activities like walking or gardening tend to develop only one of the above fitness components. You will not significantly develop strength, flexibility, aerobic capacity or attain your optimum body-fat composition just by walking, for instance – you will need a balanced exercise programme to do this. When taking up a comprehensive exercise programme, make sure you get professional instruction and adopt a programme that is suitable for your age and physical condition. Check with your doctor if you are unsure of your health.

What regular walking and gardening *will* give you is a healthy lifestyle. You will be healthy but not fit. A sedentary person (one that sits all day) will be neither fit nor healthy. As the first Greek physician, Hippocrates, said: 'A body that does not exercise is a sick body.' Two and a half thousand years later, this is still true!

The cheapest exercise of all is walking. You don't need to join a club, and the road has never been known to run out! The most pleasurable exercise – and the most natural – is lovemaking! Research shows that people who indulge themselves in this 'exercise programme' have less heart disease and stress! So if you ever needed an excuse to have sex, now is the time!

Those who exercise regularly will:

- enjoy a longer life
- be more healthy
- have fewer flus and colds

- have more energy
- keep the ageing process at bay

Enjoy an activity with a family member – and make your family happier! They say that the family that prays together stays together. Well, the same could be said about exercise and activity! If you share outside activity together you will be far more likely to enjoy the activity to the full and stick to your activity programme. Walking, swimming, gardening or hill-climbing together can only develop and strengthen bonds.

Which member of my family can I share an activity with?
Tick the appropriate Family Member and approach them gently with the suggestion!

Partner or spouse	☐
Mum	☐
Dad	☐
Son	☐
Daughter	☐
Sister	☐
Brother	☐
Grandparent	☐

And if none of the above are available, why not pick a friend?

Name of friend:

What sort of activity can we share?

| Walking | ☐ |
| A recreational sport | ☐ |

(fill in which one):

Gardening ☐

Yoga ☐

Dancing ☐

Or another:

When can we do it?

am ☐

pm ☐

Monday ☐

Tuesday ☐

Wednesday ☐

Thursday ☐

Friday ☐

Saturday ☐

Sunday ☐

Making Decisions

Therapists around the world have found that consciously making decisions – especially small decisions that need to be made, like deciding to take a walk even though it is raining – will help you climb out of crisis and depression. Think of each decision as a step up towards the light. It gets you going. It gets the day started. If you are stuck in a rut, making and sticking to small decisions is the way back to sanity. It is the way to get back into the flow of life. But making decisions is hard.

Why making decisions is so hard

The word 'decide' shares a root with the words 'suicide' and 'patricide'. The '-cide' part of these words comes from the Greek, meaning 'slay' or 'kill'. Part of making decisions means that you have to 'kill' all other options available to you. For example, if you are in a relationship that is turning sour, you know you should end it. But that means you will have killed off the current relationship – and possibly any chance of it working out in the future. Now this is a big risk, especially when you consider that most people are fearful of change. (That is why so many couples go back into abusive relationships: they fear change.) No wonder it is difficult to make decisions – you are 'murdering' your options!

The danger of indecision

As a result of all this, people faced with tough decisions tend to be indecisive. This may work in their favour in the short term: they keep all their options alive. But in the long term they are worse off, because options have a limited shelf-life. For example, the new job offer you receive will not last forever – it will eventually be filled by someone else if you do not make a decision. Just as that dishy person in the office who has been making eyes at you will eventually find someone else if you sit on the fence too long and ignore them.

The truth is that the opportunity of a lifetime must be taken in the lifetime of the opportunity. And that means making decisions. So as we go through the seven steps to a happier family, you have to make decisions, otherwise nothing will change.

Let's face our first decision in our seven-step programme to having a happier family. Let's make a decision on having activity in our family life. And remember, not making a decision is a decision in itself: it is allowing life to pass you by.

When you have made a decision on having a healthier family, write it down.

The importance of writing decisions down

When you get married or buy a house, you have to commit your decision to paper. Now there is an ancient wisdom in all this: writing something down makes it more concrete – more real – than just leaving it as an idea floating round in your head. Writing it down is like taking a snapshot. It is the photograph of the moment of decision. That is why we have left space in the book for you to write down your decisions.

If you are not comfortable writing personal decisions in this book, buy a notebook or find a scrap of paper and write it down there.

Remember: Always write your decisions down!

Before we make a decision on whether we will have an active family or not, let's recap on the main points:

Seven Tips for Having a Healthy Body

- Take up physical activity that you enjoy
- Do it as often as you can – at least three times a week
- Work the heart and lungs – exert yourself enough to get mildly out of breath and break into a light sweat
- Choose an activity that uses all the body's major muscle groups and makes the body go through the largest range of movements
- Join a gym and start a supervised fitness programme
- Do your activity with a family member or friend, if you can – it always helps!
- Take medical advice before starting anything strenuous, and check up on your family's medical history

Remember, if you want to have a happy family, you need to have a healthy family.

My decision on becoming part of an active family

Fill in the gaps:

I will   with   at   every

Good luck! You have now completed the first step to having a happier family!

Step 2
Having a Healthy Spirit

The Greeks believed we were made up of two things: a body that we can see and a spirit that gives us life but can't be seen. We know we must have a healthy body in order to enjoy a happy family life. We also need a healthy spirit.

What is a healthy spirit?

The word 'spirit' comes from the Latin 'spiritus', which means 'that which animates us'. It is the invisible part of you – the part that gives you life. How 'happy' your spirit is will determine how happy your family life is. It will also determine how you view the world, what your place in the universe is and how optimistic you are about life, death, God and 'life after death'. Moreover, it will inform your moral views on life: your ability to distinguish right from wrong.

Your spiritual health determines how you experience life and how you behave in life. If your spirit is unhealthy, then so are you! If you are filled with light, then others will see it. The problem is that our universe is made up of both light and dark – and so are our personalities. Being spiritually healthy is a very personal thing, and different people have different definitions of spiritual health. One definition that is universally popular is the concept of light and darkness representing good and evil in a person's life. In this instance, being spiritually healthy involves not allowing the inner light of your soul to be swamped by the darkness of severe depression, drug addiction, alcoholism, anger or regret. For with the light we can see our way forward, whereas if we are filled with darkness we will lose our way and stumble and fall into the abyss.

So let's examine how healthy our spirit is.

How healthy is my spirit? How filled with light is it?

In the chart on the next page, put a tick under the appropriate number, and at the end you will get some idea of how healthy your spirit is.

Remember, gauging your spiritual health is a lot more difficult than gauging your physical health. For one thing, it is far more personal. For example, some people can be perfectly happy without ever believing in God, fate or an afterlife. They can still live full and moral lives ('moral' meaning 'distinguishing between right and wrong').

On the other hand, those who purport to have high moral standards and appear to be living exemplary lives can in fact be living a lie. The number of people in Ireland who have been convicted of child abuse while in positions of moral authority is a sobering examples of this. In this sense, your spiritual health also determines how truthful you are, both to yourself and to others.

| | Healthy | | | | | | | | | | Unhealthy |
| --- | 10 | 9 | 8 | 7 | 6 | 5 | 4 | 3 | 2 | 1 | 0 |

I feel loved by some greater power that looks after me in many ways, even when things go wrong

On balance, I am glad to be alive – even though I sometimes feel sad or despairing

Every day, I try to tell the difference between right and wrong, and live my life accordingly

I feel I am connected to everything else in the universe. I am not alone, even though I can sometimes feel lonely

I feel great wonder at life in all its many forms

I take time out every day for myself, just to ponder on life, the universe and my place within it

I am able to ask forgiveness for the hurts I have caused others

I am able to forgive those who have hurt me

On the whole, I am truthful and honest, both to myself and to others

Those who know me best would agree that I am truthful and honest, both to myself and to others

Now join up the dots to create a rough guide to your spiritual health. Are you spiritually healthy? If you gave more than four 'No' answers, you may want to take stock of your spiritual health, and if you think you need help in a particular area, speak to your GP, a trusted friend, a mentor, a therapist or a spiritual director. A sympathetic priest, rector or rabbi can also be of help.

The importance of consulting your GP

Remember, depression in its many forms can lead to feelings of spiritual depression and isolation. People suffering from depression feel the two 'H's – hopelessness and helplessness – and believe they are cut off from life and the real world. They also invariably blame themselves for this situation, whereas it is in fact a result of a medical condition that can be treated with therapy and medication. If you are feeling cut off from life and unable to cope, help is at hand: consult your GP!

The Celtic Tiger v. spirituality

As we in Ireland become more materially successful (some would say obsessed with wealth), we may lose sight of our spiritual health. In Ireland, this has coincided with a sharp decline in religious practice, due in part to the scandals that have rocked the Catholic Church. A recent survey showed that only 14 per cent of young people believed that going to Mass was important nowadays.

So where does that leave us – and particularly young people?

Some would say that this leaves a gaping hole which organised religion no longer fills. But this can be dangerous, for as any scientist will tell you, a vacuum is quickly filled – with consumerism, experimenting with drugs, alcoholism, casual sex, pornography, violent behaviour, or indeed anything that gives you a feeling of being stimulated, connected and appreciated, whether it is healthy or not.

But despite the decline in religious practice on the part of many in Ireland, there is still a widespread interest in spiritual things in Ireland. People are trying alternative religions and philosophies. Human beings need to experience the spiritual in the widest sense of the word. The problem is how to get that spiritual experience in today's hectic world, when we hardly have time for ourselves and our children, let alone any higher power.

A guiding power

Below are some suggestions on how to find your spiritual self. We can be optimistic, for if there is a guiding power (however we define it) in the universe, it will help guide us through life, no matter what. And then there are such things as serendipity, synchronicity and sudden, unexpected blessings.

There is also intuition and that old-fashioned word 'conscience', which is derived from the Latin for 'to be with knowing'. Often, we will know in our hearts what we should do – and know the difficult steps we must take to do what needs to be done. The problem then lies in having the courage and discipline to take these steps!

Below are some ways in which you can nourish and protect your spiritual health.

1: Find quiet time for yourself

The members of the early monastic settlements in Ireland all knew one thing: there must be quiet times in the day if you are to be spiritually healthy.

Now ask yourself the following questions:

Where are my quiet times in the daily round?
Do I have any?
And if I do, how do I spend them?

Here are a few suggestions on how to find quiet time for yourself.

Finding quiet times

- Instead of taking the car all the way into work, park and walk the final part. This will allow you time for yourself. Do the same on your way home
- If you take a bus or train to work, get off one or two stops before your usual stop and walk the rest of the way
- At lunch, take ten to fifteen minutes of quiet time for yourself
- In the evening time, take a walk to the local park, or take the dog around the block
- Light a scented candle and make a special place for yourself in a room. Put on quiet music (wave or dolphin sounds are available on tape or CD) and listen to your breathing
- Buy a relaxation tape
- Learn to meditate or take yoga classes

- Have a massage
- Pop into a church at any time and just sit quietly under a favourite painting or statue. This spiritual setting can help transport you out of your present stressful existence into a realm of reflective peace
- Walk by the sea
- Occasionally take a day off and walk the Sugar Loaf Mountain or country spot, or find a deserted beach or strand
- Change your annual holiday and visit one of the many holy sites around the world (from the Pyramids, to Fatima, to the River Ganges in India). This will help change your entire perspective on life. (I visited Jerusalem and Bethlehem one Christmas and found it one of the great inspirations and revelations of my life. It taught me a lot about the three great world religions and how they regard each other.)

Now take the time to think about how you can make quiet time for yourself. If you decide you want quiet time, write down when you will take it and how you will spend it.

I can find quiet time at the following times:

am	☐
pm	☐
Monday	☐
Tuesday	☐
Wednesday	☐
Thursday	☐
Friday	☐
Saturday	☐
Sunday	☐

Where will I have my quiet time? (tick)

Home
Organise a quiet room ☐
Walk in neighbourhood ☐

Work
Lunchtime ☐
On my way into/home from work ☐

If I could take a 'spiritual holiday',
I would go to   (fill in).

2: *Find Fellowship*

Unless you are one of the thirty-seven registered hermits in Ireland, you need people around you!

One of the reasons older people fall into depression is that they become increasingly isolated as they get older and their friends die. Isolation breeds depression. (Remember, the greatest punishment in prison is for the person to be deprived of company and put in solitary confinement.)

So how do I go about getting fellowship that will help my spiritual health?

Attend a formal religious service

There are plenty of such services in Ireland – just turn up any Sunday morning at your local church! The problem here is that familiarity breeds contempt. If you are finding your local service in some ways too familiar, you can always get the bus into town and try another church or denomination. There are a many available, and they can give you a new slant on old ideas. You can also try out the local mosque or synagogue. Most welcome strangers to their celebrations. Ring beforehand and find out.

I have visited all sorts of churches and spiritual places of worship, from fundamentalist gatherings to St Peter's in Rome, from mosques to synagogues and Buddhist temples, and found that all of them had something to say. You don't have to join the particular religion, but the experience will get you thinking, and give you interaction with other people.

3: Find the guidance of a mentor during a spiritual crisis

A mentor is someone who helps you on your path through life. They can be your mum, a friendly uncle or a total stranger you meet on the train. Mentors are there to help you overcome the trials of life, be it a broken romance, a failing marriage, unemployment, depression, difficulties at work, finally death, bereavement or ill health. The mentor is helpful because he or she has already been through such an experience.

How to tell a good mentor from a bad one

A good mentor does not tell you what to do! Rather, he or she helps you make decisions for yourself. That way, *you* become spiritually strong.

But don't worry about finding a mentor: at the right time, *they* will find *you!*

4: Find the company of like-minded people who have suffered the same setbacks as you

You can also nourish your spiritual growth by spending time in the company of like-minded people who have experienced the same thing as you are going through. These are the sort of people who don't tell you what to do, or how wrong you have been. They know what it is like to make terrible mistakes and they will give support, not condemnation.

AA is a shining example of such a group. The first thing about an AA group is that it has no leader. The second is that all of those who attend know that they are just one drink away from falling into hopeless addiction again.

Find a group of people who have suffered the same problems as you – be it divorce, depression, abuse, neglect, bereavement or loss. There are many such groups nowadays and the front of the telephone directory or directory enquiries will have their number.

Fellowship of this sort is vital for your emotional and spiritual well-being and can fill the gap that family and friends cannot, because of their lack of experience of the particular problem. In such circumstances, this type of group becomes especially important, because it remains outside the tight family circle and all that that entails. Also, what goes on in a session is treated with the utmost confidence and will never be flung back at you, as can happen in families when things go wrong.

Once you have looked after your own spiritual health, you can begin to look at your family's spiritual health and find ways to improve it.

Happy Families - How to Make Them Spiritually Strong

We have already quoted the old saying: 'The family that prays together, stays together.'

Nowadays, research shows that families are no longer praying together. Just ask yourself how many families you know that pray together at mealtimes? Can you think of a dozen? Can you think of even one?

I can't. The families I know are scattered around the TV at mealtimes, playing videos, chatting or listening to CDs. It would not enter their heads to thank God for the food they are about to receive. In fact, the children hardly even thank their mum, who has prepared it! And that brings us to a thorny question: if young people (and old ones, for that matter) will not willingly pray at mealtimes or on Sundays, should we make them?

Coercion and Religion: Making People Pray

Forty years ago, the vast majority of people in Ireland (both teenagers and adults) were forced to go to Mass, either by their parents or by peer pressure. The thinking was that this would make them devout Catholics for life. But take away the coercion, and what happens? The numbers of people attending Mass drop dramatically. According to the most recent research, only 14 per cent of teenagers go to Mass, and the proportion of adults who attend Mass has plummeted.

What chains need breaking in your life?

Does coercion work as a long-term policy?

Think back to your own childhood experiences. Did coercion work for you in the long term? Do you now read Shakespeare because you were forced to do it at school? Do you now speak Irish for the same reason? Let's look at things in reverse, as most coercion is about making people *not* do things. Do you abstain from alcohol or smoking because it was forbidden when you were young? Do you abstain from extramarital sex because it was forbidden? The answer is probably no. Most of us go on to assert ourselves as adults, and we only stop drinking, smoking or having extramarital sex if we decide to do so.

Coercion has a poor record of success as a way of modifying people's behaviour. Look at the Soviet Union, where people were coerced into doing and thinking all sorts of things. The system inevitably collapsed under it own inconsistencies and people soon stopped doing all the things they had been forced to do under the oppressive regime. Coercion does not really work. In fact, forcing people to do anything is usually counter-productive. Think of your own experience: do you like being pushed around and told you *must* do something when you may not see the point of it? Most people would rather make up their own minds.

So how does a modern family voluntarily pray together?

That is a difficult question to answer. Many family members are too busy to be interested in their spiritual health. But here are some fresh suggestions for those who may taken an interest in spiritual well-being:

- Take the family for a walk on a Sunday morning, in the park or on the beach, and bring up questions of life, life after death, the universe, nature and our place within it. It could prove to be a stimulating, informative and even spiritual conversation
- Go as a family and spend some quiet time in church. Light a candle and pray for something the whole family wants to happen
- Read and discuss stories from the Bible or other spiritual texts, or watch films that have a spiritual content, like *The Mission*
- Talk as a family and ask questions. For example: how would the children like to spend their Sunday mornings? How important is God in their lives? What is their understanding of God?

If you can make spirituality interesting, children will respond and you will have an interesting discussion.

Now, see if you can select some ways in which your family can celebrate its spirituality:

Time:
Place:
Activity:

5: Nourish Your Spirit

We need spiritual food if we are to flourish. This means that we have to find ways of feeding our spirits.

Below are several ways in which you can feed your own spirit and that of your family:

Attend specific religious or spiritual services

These can range from a traditional Latin Mass to a sweat lodge in the Wicklow Mountains! A sweat lodge is an old American Indian way of cleansing the spirit. You sit as naked as you can tolerate and sweat it out in total darkness, while the body and spirit is cleansed of impurities. (Catholics have Confession – where you get to keep your clothes on! Having tried only the latter, I am not sure which is more fun.)

There are now so may sorts of religious and spiritual practices – from Pagan ceremonies, to ancient Druid worship, Eastern mysticism and modern-day Christianity – in Ireland that one is spoiled for choice.

Attend courses inospirituality

There are now courses available in every subject under the sun: from the teachings of Thomas Aquinas, to Zen Buddhism, to how Fung Shui can change your life.

You can attend courses at weekends or in the evenings, at a university or in the local healing centre or parish hall. There are one-day courses, weekend courses, part-time courses and full-time courses in a wide range of subjects, and some courses can even lead to qualifications and degrees.

Read about spirituality

This is perhaps the most informative and convenient way to learn about spirituality! Remember, the teachings of all the great world religions were first written in books: the Bible, the Torah and the Koran.

If you have access to a local library, a world of spirituality is at your fingertips. If you have the money, the local bookstore can order you any book in the world!

There is no longer any barrier to you feeding your spirit. And if you have access to the Internet, you could spend several lifetimes browsing the wealth of information contained there.

But do not be too quick to look for books – let them find you! From the moment St Augustine took to letting the Bible fall open at any page and finding a personal message therein, people have been sought out by books with messages looking for owners with a corresponding need!

They say that for every spiritual crisis in your life, there is a book waiting with a message of help. So walk down to the local library or bookshop and begin to browse. Within ten minutes, I guarantee you will be reading something of relevance to your situation.

Books are angels in disguise, so it is said. Not only can they feed your spirit – they can help lead you out of a crisis! But don't believe me – go out and try it for yourself!

Other ways to nourish your spirit

Writing

Treat yourself to a journal or a simple notebook and begin jotting down your musings on life, the universe and anything else that comes into your mind. Don't edit your writing or try to sound deep and meaningful. Simply write – a piece of paper never refused ink! If you give yourself just ten minutes a day to write, and do it daily, you will be amazed at what comes out.

Keep in mind Julia Cameron's advice in her excellent book *The Writer's Way:* just write continuous stream-of-consciousness thoughts without pausing to see how it reads. Don't worry about spelling, or how it all sounds – just write! In years to come, you will have a true snapshot of how you felt at that particular time.

Find a writing companion

Then find a friend who you can trust, and read out extracts to them. Perhaps they will begin to write as well and you will have a true companion! Writing honestly and from the heart can really liberate feelings that need liberation; I can think of few things that will free your spirit more.

Develop an interest in philosophy

Philosophy is the study of life and meaning – and the wonder of life. As Plato wrote, a person who does not wonder at life is a dead person. Study or read about philosophy and it will help you ask the right questions. It may also help you find the right answers!

The same could be said about studying the history of religion, on which there are many courses. Consult your local guide to evening classes.

Learn how to meditate

Meditation will feed your spirit and help you deal with stress. It is a great way of finding quietness in the middle of noise and confusion. There are many forms of meditation, from Christian meditation to Zen Buddhism. Try them all until you find one that suits you.

Alternative therapies

Every year I have a stand at the mind, body, spirit exhibition at the RDS, Dublin, where I sell my books and tapes. Here I see alternative forms of therapy and spiritual development – from the study of past lives, to healing crystals and tarot-card readings. Look out for the exhibition – it falls on St Patrick's weekend – and come along and see for yourself. (Make sure to look me up if you do!) There are now similar exhibitions around the country. Check them out.

Finally, if you find you are struggling with your spiritual health, consult your local priest or minister, or find a counsellor you can trust. Shop around till you are happy, and remember that the right person will present themselves when the time is right.

Step 3
Developing your Emotional Health

The buzz phrase of the 1990s was 'emotional intelligence'. The term was coined by the writer Daniel Goldman, whose book *Emotional Intelligence* popularised the concept. The arrival of emotional intelligence righted the balance that had previously favoured one kind of intelligence over another. Goldman showed that there were over twenty forms of intelligence, and this discovery broke the mould. Before that, traditional IQ – left-brain, cognitive and rational thinking – ruled the roost. Now we know that children can be blessed with many sorts of intelligence, from interpersonal IQ, (the ability to see how people interact with each another) to intrapersonal IQ (the ability to know how your emotions work).

Unfortunately, Ireland's Leaving and Junior Cert exams reward only traditional IQ, while leaving those who are gifted in other areas unrewarded. That is why many of the leading lights in this country – writers, artists, entrepreneurs, businessmen, entertainers and sportsmen and women – often fail to shine in the Leaving Cert or lose interest in excelling, even when they could. This is wrong. It is like rewarding only people with blue eyes: it does not make sense. Green, brown and grey eyes can all see just as well; they are just different!

Helping your children discover their own unique intelligence

Your child could be a genius without knowing it – and so could you! It is important that your children know this fact, and it is important that you know it too. If you are aware of this, you can immediately help your family excel in areas where they are strong by encouraging them in all they do, especially if it falls outside normal academic subjects.

Unfortunately, we are in the habit of berating children and young adults who are not sufficiently clever or bookish in the traditional academic sense. This should stop.

Just look at this list of Irish people who did not excel at 'book' learning or were not very interested in it. Are they unsuccessful?

Paul McGuinness, manager of U2
Denis O'Brien, founder of Esat
Sonia O'Sullivan, runner
Louis Walsh, manager of Boyzone and other international acts
Bono, lead singer of U2 and key organiser of Jubilee 2000
        (campaigning for Third World debt reduction)
Roy Keane, captain of Manchester United
Philip Tracey, international hat designer
Gabriel Byrne, Hollywood film star
Liam Neeson, Oscar nominee

. . . and the dozens of Irish entrepreneurs who have started up successful businesses and e-commerce or dot-com companies in the last decade, many of which are now multimillion-pound enterprises.

Interesting fact

Research shows that people with high IQs in the traditional sense will end up working for those with lower IQs. It is only when you come to test the latter using other criteria that you discover they are significantly talented in other areas, such as people-handling, seeing through a problem or taking on a task that would terrify most people! All this means only one thing: the traditional IQ test is very lopsided!

Research also shows that people with high IQs are more introverted and have greater problems with forming and keeping relationships. Being 'clever' in the old-fashioned sense of the word has its drawbacks!

Helping yourself or your partner discover your own unique intelligence

The same rule applies to husbands, wives and partners. Earlier in life, they may have settled for a career for which they were not suited. It is difficult to be happy if you are in the wrong career, and it is never too late to learn, retrain and change. (We will be helping you find your ideal career or job in Step 6.)

Other Ways in which you and your family can work on your Emotional Health

Learning to listen to one another

Interesting facts

Research shows that most people never really listen to each other. Instead, they do one of two things in conversations: immediately talk about their own experiences or give you their own opinion on the subject you are discussing.

For example, say you are telling a friend that you were thinking of buying a new Japanese car. They would respond either by telling you in detail how they had once bought a Japanese car themselves and what it was like, or by letting you know what they think about Japanese cars in general and the sort of car you *should* buy.

The truth is that people rarely listen to one another. In fact, quite the opposite is true. They take up the conversation you started and monopolise it for their own ends.

Listening exercise: is anybody there?

Phone a friend and try the following, either over coffee or during the phone conversation. Start telling your friend that you are going to go on a diet or quit smoking or drinking, and try to see just how far you get before you are interrupted.

If you get to the point in the conversation – say sixty to ninety seconds in – where you are giving the reasons why you are giving up, and you have not been interrupted by the person telling you their own experiences of dieting, then hold on to that friend. They are that rare thing: a good listener!

But they are more likely to interrupt you at the first opportunity to speak about all the times they have been on a diet or to tell you their opinions on diets and why you should or should not go on one!

What you can guarantee with most people is that you will never finish your conversation!

Fascinating facts

Dr Carl Rogers of the University of Chicago did some fascinating research in the 1950s and 1960s. He found that people who were listened to without interruption or advice figure out an answer to their problem themselves and find a way to implement that solution.

He called this sort of listening 'empathetic listening', which means that the listener becomes so tuned in to what the person is saying that they almost feel what it would be like to be that person. His research formed the basis of client-centred therapy and is the basis for much of the therapy being conducted today.

Empathetic or total listening

Empathetic or total listening allows people to get to the bottom of a problem that is irritating them. Before they were listened to empathetically, they felt the problem only as a vague but annoying anxiety in the pit of their stomach, or as a nagging headache. But once the person was allowed to talk about their anxiety, it clarified into a particular issue, with a possible solution or course of action. This is what used to be called 'talking a problem out'. Research shows that this is a definite process with a series of specific steps.

1: Identifying the problem

You may have a label for your problem but not realise the full extent of how it is affecting you. The reason for this is simple: we have to suppress our problems just to get through the day and survive. If you were to tell a work colleague how you really felt about things while travelling in the lift, you would never get out!

People get into the habit of saying 'I'm fine!' or 'Couldn't be better!' just to get through the day. The problem with this is that the issues or problems begin to stack up like planes over a busy airport. If they are not eventually addressed, they will crash! Studies show that, if you suppress a problem, you make it worse, not better.

For example, consider this true-life story: 'When Harry Met Sinéad'. Harry was engaged to Sinéad, but it broke up one Christmas. Now Christmas of the following year is approaching and Harry is feeling a sudden and strange depression settle over him, which he cannot shake off. He has a new girlfriend, Mary, to whom he has just got engaged, so he cannot discuss his feelings with her for fear of upsetting her. He is determined that his second engagement will not be broken like his first, and is sure he loves Mary, so he cannot understand why he is suddenly so unhappy and thinking about Sinéad. Harry is in a bad fix.

Interesting facts

Here are some of the steps we often take to 'fix' difficult emotional problems:

- We deny the problem exists, living in a fantasy world of denial, often reverting to unrealistic 'positive thinking'

83

- We numb the problem with drink, cigarettes or whatever works
- We distract ourselves from it with work, sex, TV or busyness
- We force ourselves to work on, regardless of how painful the problem really is, believing it will go away in the end
- We rally friends to our support and form an opposing camp to the 'enemy' – the ex-boyfriend, former boss, hated brother or despised mother – often taking solace while damning our enemies
- We seek the advice of friends and then try to follow that advice, however impractical, painful or ridiculous it may be. If it all goes wrong in the end, we can blame them!

Rarely do we sit down and address the problem it all its seriousness, trying to learn where we ourselves went wrong. Nor do we seek professional help, even though the problem may be negatively affecting our work, health and family life. (If it was a new car, we would have called in the mechanic the first time we heard a rattle!)

2: Denying the problem we know we have!

Interestingly, we often immediately try to deny we have a problem, even after we have acknowledged it! This is a common pattern with alcoholics, who have a moment of truth immediately covered by the cloak of self-delusion. But as they joke in psychology: de-nial is not a river in Egypt!

The Dangers of Denial

Denying something won't make it go away. In the short term we get relief, but it only puts the problem on the long finger. Meanwhile, like a bad tooth, it gets worse and can end up poisoning the whole system. In the end, the pain will get too much and it will ultimately drive us to seek help.

Example: When Harry met Sinéad

Harry cannot explain his sudden depression. He was convinced he had gotten over Sinéad and is sure he is head over heels in love with Mary – that was, until this black feeling suddenly settled over him, a feeling he could not shake off, and images of Sinéad began to haunt him again.

He began drinking late at night, just to numb the feeling, but his fiancée, Mary, began to complain and they began rowing. Now he was feeling even worse. At home he was short-tempered and irritable, while at work he was distracted and unfocused. People began to ask questions about his commitment to the sales team he ran, and the sales figures began to flag. This flung him into further depression and more drinking.

One night, when he was really drunk, he blurted out to Mary that he was still thinking about Sinéad. Mary was deeply upset and stormed off, flinging the engagement ring at him, but the next time they met she had calmed down. She told Harry she had talked to her mother and her mother had a suggestion. Her friend was a counsellor who would see Harry if he agreed. At first Harry rejected the idea out of hand, begging Mary to come back to him. But Mary would not think about coming back until he promised to go for at least one counselling session. Harry eventually agreed, rather than lose Mary. In fact, he was secretly glad of the chance to get help: the pain was eating him up.

3: Being Heard: the Onion-Layers effect

Starting the process of problem-solving

Fascinating fact: Repeating what the speaker says

Dr Carl Rogers discovered that when we are listened to empathetically, a series of layers to our problem begin to peel off, like the skins of an onion, slowly revealing the real problem at the centre. The longer we are listened to, the more skins get peeled back. The key to this peeling back is remarkably simple: the listener must repeat back to the speaker the gist of what he has just heard. This enables the speaker to check whether he is right in what he is thinking , just as you would look at yourself in the mirror before buying a jacket, to see if it looks right. This self-reflection is essential if you are to get to the bottom of your problem. But the process is delicate: it can be sabotaged the moment the listener talks about his own experiences or offers advice.

If you find a friend who can listen to you empathetically or go to a therapist trained in empathetic listening, the following things will happen as you talk about your problem. You will start with either a well-worn idea of the problem if it is an old one, or a just a vague sense of unease if it is a new problem. As you talk it through and the listener repeats back the key things you are saying, the layers begin to peel back, and you start to see why you are so worried, upset or on edge.

When Harry met Sinéad

Harry sits down with the counsellor who asks him what the problem is. In this extract from a real case (in which the name and details have been changed), Harry outlines the details of his relationship with and engagement to Sinéad, followed by the break-up and cancelling of the engagement. He then talks about how he was fine for ten months, during which time he formed a new relationship with Mary and got engaged again. Then, however, depression hit him out of the blue, just four weeks before Christmas, causing the heavy drinking and rowing.

> *T = Therapist*
> *H = Harry*

T: Have you any idea what the black feeling is about?

H: Not really. I thought I was over Sinéad. Then I saw the Christmas decorations in Grafton Street – and suddenly it got to me.

T: The decorations in Grafton Street upset you?

H: Yes. It was about this time last year we bought the engagement ring. [long pause] The decorations on the street had just gone up then as well.

T: The decorations reminded you of buying the engagement ring with Sinéad?

H: I guess so [quietly]. We had a great day. We met her sister afterwards and went to Sinéad's house to announce the news . . . [voice falters]

T: You went home and told them about the engagement?

H: [tears fill his eyes] Yes, Sinéad's mum was delighted. Her dad too. They openned a bottle of bubbly, and the sisters came round – real happy families!

T: So you celebrated your engagement with her family.

H: Yep. [pauses, deep in thought] She was looking really good that day – she had on a red top I'd got her when we were on holidays. [long pause] She said we would always be together, held my hand . . . [tears start again] Her mum said she had made the right choice.

T: Her Mum said she had made a good choice picking you?

H: [voice husky] Yes . . . and I thought that was it – I thought I had meet the person I would spend the rest of my life with.

T: You did?

H: Yes – but two months later, it was all off. She wanted to put the wedding off until after we'd gone to Australia for a year, and I would have none of it – couldn't leave the job – had too much on. I said we'd get married first and go the following year – though I didn't really want to. I had changed my mind and she knew it . . . we had a row.

T: What happened?

H: She said that if I was going to act like that before we got married, what would I be like when we *were* married. I stormed out, called it off.

T: You called it off?

H: [shakes head] Yep – stupidest thing I ever did. When I crawled back to her three weeks later, she had gone!

T: Gone?

H: Yeah – bloody left for Australia. Never even told me.

T: She never even told you she was going?

H: Not a bloody word, just upped and left. I felt a right idiot.

A Happy Relationship is....

T: What you do then?

H: My whole life crashed. It was as if I she'd shot me. I drank. I moped for a couple of months and then I meet Mary.

T: How did that go?

H: I think I was lonely. We got on well. Mary was keen on me. She pursued me, if you know what I mean. I'd be all alone for the evening and she'd ring or call round. I suppose I got used to the attention.

T: You got used to the attention?

H: Yeah, I was flattered.

T: So you got engaged?

H: Yep . . . [tears] Though now, I think it was partly out of revenge.

T: Revenge?

H: Yeah. I know this sounds weird, but I wanted Sinéad to know that I didn't care about her any more.

T: You wanted her to know you didn't care?

H: Yep. I loved Mary. I'd found a new girl. [places hands on head] I wanted Sinéad to suffer.

T: You wanted her to suffer?

H: Yep – for what she did.

T: And what was that, Harry?

H: She f****** off. Left me high and dry. Made me look like an idiot. [long pause, with tears] But I still missed her. I missed her terribly.

T: You missed her – like in the past? You missed her then but not now?

H: [crying, and deeply upset] No, I miss her *now!*

T: You miss her now?

H: [shakes head slowly] Yep, and it's killing me.

T: It is?

H: [nods]

T: And what about Mary?

H: What about her?

T: What are you going to do about her? She loves you and thinks you're going to marry her.

H: [shakes head] I don't know . . .

T: You think you can go ahead with it?

H: [long pause] No, not if I'm honest. You see, I don't know if I love Mary. When it comes to the crunch – when I think of marrying her – I panic.

T: You panic?

H: Yeah.

T: [pause] And how does that feel – panicking?

H: Bad.

T: And are you still planning to marry her – even though you feel panic?

H: [shakes head] I don't think so . . .

T: Why not?

H: [pause] It wouldn't be fair.

T: Marrying Mary wouldn't be fair?

H: No.

T: So what would be fair, Harry?

H: [deep sigh] Tell her the truth – break off the engagement. It'll break her heart, but it's better this way.

T: It's better to break off the engagement and end the relationship?

H: Yes, I think so. It's the right thing to do. The only thing. Can't play her along.

T: You can't do that?

H: [shakes his head] No.

T: And Sinéad?

H: [smiles grimly] That's a hard one. She's in Australia – what the f*** can I do?

T: You don't know what to do?

H: No!

T: But the engagement with Mary must be called off –
       you're sure of that?

H: And soon – otherwise I'll go soft.

T: You've got to do it soon?

H: F****** sure, or she'll start at me again and I'll mess
       the whole thing up.

T: And you don't want to do that?

H: No!

This first session was a major breakthrough for Harry, who did call off his engagement with Mary. For a while, his drinking worsened and he was threatened with the sack from work. But after fourteen weeks of seeing his therapist once a week, Harry began to see the light at the end of the tunnel. He manage to contact Sinéad, who told him she had got engaged to an Australian and was settling there. It was not a good conversation. Harry's drinking worsened again for a while and he went back to his therapist, and from there onto a support group for alcoholics and relatives of alcoholics, where he met his future wife. He is now settled, but he still sees his therapist when the dark clouds gather. He also regularly attends the support group with his wife.

Lessons we can learn from Harry

Harry made such a leap because he was listened to completely. He had a problem and was allowed to uncover it by the attitude the listener took. If the listener had made the usual response of someone in conversation, Harry could never have gotten to a point of resolution on that first session, because his companion would either have talked about her own relationship problems or have worn him down with well-intentioned advice as to why he should do this or that.

You too can learn to listen. Just follow these tips while listening to a friend or family member who has something on their mind. (Remember, 'total listening' is only appropriate for someone who has a problem they need to thrash out. All details should be treated in the utmost confidence, or the person will never trust you again.) As a 'total listener', you must:

- Learn to button up your lips and never share advice – this will stop the process!
- Never go into your history while engaged in total listening. If you do, the speaker will stop following his own process and begin following yours.
- Practise. For those who have no experience of total listening, it is difficult to endure the sudden silences that fill the conversation as the speaker begins to unravel the jumble of their thoughts and emotions. People are uncomfortable with silence and will say anything just to cover it up. But it is that very silence that allows the speaker to see through the jumble of their own life, and start to make sense of it. If you speak, you will destroy the process of the person making sense of their problem.
- Join a counselling course or take up a form of listening therapy yourself. Alternatively, find a friend and go through the exercises I have listed in my book *Everyday Genius.*

Focusing – the art of developing your emotional IQ

Fascinating fact: the importance of feeling

Researchers have found that we make the major decisions in our life – e.g. getting into or out of a relationship, buying a house or changing jobs or cars – using a non-verbal, gut feeling. For example, you may suddenly feel that a relationship is no longer working and decide to end it. Immediately, you rationalise your decision, coming up with all kinds of logic and reasons: 'I never really liked him/her', 'We didn't really have anything in common', 'His family would never have accepted me'.

The researchers found that this rationalisation, or 'excuse-making', while true to some degree, was not the real reason the person made the change! The reason was found in the 'feeling' that the job or relationship was no longer working. That is why it is virtually impossible to make a lover understand why you are leaving them, because the decision was made primarily by feeling and was non-verbal. Trying to put it into words is doomed to failure – and will probably only make things worse!

So how can we regularly access our feelings?

Professor Eugene Gendlin of the University of Chicago spent his entire life researching feelings and emotional problems. He came up with some fascinating conclusions in this area. (You can read these at length in his book *Focusing*, published by Bantam Press, or in my book *Everyday Genius*. Also, you can contact the Web site of the Focusing Institute, New York, where the results of over sixty trials and studies on focusing and listening are available on: www.focusing.org .)

Professor Gendlin discovered that there is a natural process we all have for accessing and solving emotional problems. He called it 'focusing'. Many of us have forgotten how to focus. This is because focusing is experienced as a bodily sensation or feeling. For example, think of the person you most dislike. Now imagine that that person happened to come into the room and sit down next to you. What would that do to your body? Your feelings? Your stomach and heart rate? Your well-being?

Now you can see or feel the difference between the two forms of knowing – the two forms of intelligence. Which of the two was more immediate and real for you. Which best describes this person you most dislike?

Most people will plump for the second. The first, describing your favourite person, was an intellectual exercise, conducted mostly in your head. The second was more visceral or felt in the body, focusing on what it would be like if your least favourite person bumped into you out of the blue, such as at a party. You can try all you like to prepare for the experience of meeting someone who has hurt you, or someone who betrayed you, like a lover who cheated on you. But no mental exercise can prepare you for a face-to-face meeting, such as when you have to attend a friend's birthday party, and your ex (who cheated on you with a close friend), is going to be there with that friend.

You can try to prepare in your head for the encounter, telling yourself it is all water under the bridge and you have got over it. You arrive late, hoping against hope that the person will have left – and lo and behold, they are not there. You have a drink and start to relax, giving thanks to the heavens they have left and berating yourself for getting into such a flap over it. Then suddenly you turn round and bump into the person, spilling wine over your suit. They had forgotten the birthday present and were returning to drop it in to the host.

Suddenly your heart is pounding in your chest and your are breathing like a hyperventilating horse that has just run the Grand National. Your hands begin to shake and the words die on your lips. All your good intentions fly out of the window as the old anger, bitterness and resentment well up. You both go to say something and you stammer to a halt while your ex completes your sentence. They are far more relaxed than you. (After all, they have the love and attention of your former friend.) You feel a lump in your throat. The fact that they seem so happy and relaxed is the last straw. You snap and say something horrible at them, turn on your heel and run – all your good intentions having disappeared out the window.

The reason this sort of thing happens is simple. Experiencing the event is far more real and powerful than thinking about it – and you experience *all* events with your body. It is the home of all your senses and the receptacle for all the stimuli you react with each day. Gendlin found that the body has its own, phenomenal memory of events and logic. For instance, we have all experienced smelling just a whiff of perfume off a passer-by; those few molecules of scent can awaken a forty-year-old bodily memory, of your mother tucking you up in bed. The same can happen when you hear a snatch of music which takes you back to your first date all those years ago.

The experiences of these bodily aroused memories are far more 'real' than simply trying to remember what it was like on your first date, or how mum used to tuck you up in bed. In both cases, it is the bodily sensed 'experience' of mum, or your first date, that is evoked by the physical stimuli of perfume or music. It is something real, like perfume or music, that evokes such powerful recreations of your past. It is as if your physical memory of your mother's perfume was lying dormant till molecules of the same perfume triggered the experience of her tucking you in.

In the same way, the encounter with the ex-lover and former best friend in person triggered a violent physio-logical and emotional response, while merely 'thinking' about them – although bad enough – in no way provoked the same response.

This brings us to Gendlin's next discovery: that people experience life by living it. For example, you can read all you like about love. You can go and see all the great films ever made on it, or read all the great books written on it, or recite all the poems about it. But the only way you will really understand it is by being in love – by experiencing it! Gendlin discovered that we often try to sort out our deepest problems in our heads, in an intellectual way, whereas his research showed that all our deepest problems are experienced as feelings in our bodies.

Gendlin also discovered something profound in his therapy sessions: if you connect with the feeling of something being wrong in a certain way, you will connect with the solution! This sounds rather strange. Stay with the bad feeling about a lover that betrayed you and you will connect to the solution: are you mad? Surely you should try to get as far away from the upset feeling as possible, or eliminate it from your mind, like when you press the Delete key on the computer.

But Gendlin found that pressing 'Delete' on horrible feelings did *not* make them go away. In fact, it made them more troublesome. It seems that, when we try to get rid of difficult feelings, we simply highlight them and give them more energy. As anyone who knows about computers will tell you, it is virtually impossible to get rid of material from a computer once it is on the hard drive. Everything that has been deleted ends up in emergency back-up files. That is why the FBI can track down paedophiles who delete all their material, thinking it is gone: the material is still there, burned into the hard drive, which only a special programme can get rid of. The same is true of hurtful, painful feelings. Pressing 'Delete' only pushes these feelings deeper into the psyche, where they slowly begin to poison it. And this is where Gendlin's discovery is so helpful and exciting, for it showed that, if we focus on a horrible feeling for a while in a certain way, this feeling itself shows us the solution to the problem.

The bad feeling knows the answer!

It's a bit like sitting in a room in front of a painting and feeling uncomfortable. You know there is something wrong with the painting but you can't quite put your finger on what it is. Then, as you focus in on the painting, you see it. The picture is slightly crooked and is throwing off the symmetry of the whole room. How do you know the painting is crooked? Because you know how it should be: you know what hanging straight looks like. In fact, you can only know the painting is crooked because you know first what straight is!

It is the same with our emotional problems. We only know that something is wrong with a job or relationship because we know inside how it should be! We know we should be feeling supported, loved, cherished and looked after by our partner, but this is not happening! It is then that we feel out of sorts, depressed and 'dis-eased'. It is the same with a baby. It is only seconds out of the womb but it is already looking for warmth, food and love. Its body knows what it needs to survive: it does not have to think about it!

And that is perhaps the core of Professor Gendlin's discovery and the core of emotional intelligence: our whole body knows a relationship is abusive, or a job has run its course, or a habit is destructive, just as it knows when we need to eat, go to sleep, or take a break. And the true difference between the human species and other species lies here: other animals listen to their holistic bodily intelligence, while we often ignore it!

- We often do not sleep when our bodies tell us to
- We often do not rest when our bodies tell us to
- We often do not eat – or do not stop eating – when our bodies tell us to
- We often do not end addictive or destructive behaviour when our bodies tell us to
- We often continue with stressful behaviour, even though our bodies are screaming at us to stop!

And as a result of all this, our health suffers and we become ill.

In the same way:

- We do not quit a job, even though our body tells us it is wearing our health down
- We do not move on from a relationship, even though our body tell us it is now abusive
- We do not stop destructive habits like smoking or drinking, even though our bodies scream at us every time we put a cigarette or a drink to our lips

Gendlin found that this holistic, bodily felt intelligence is rarely wrong. It is like conscience: it knows what is best for us, just as it knew what was best for us when we were squealing infants. This bodily felt sense is part of the evolutionary instinct to survive. The problem is the perennial one with humankind: we think we know better!

This brings us to a uniquely human problem: the problem of thinking too much!

The problem of thinking too much

Human beings think too much with their heads instead of feeling life experiences with their bodies! No wonder our planet is on the verge of major catastrophe. Instead of listening to our emotional intelligence and living with nature, we follow dogma, creed, political manifestos and advertising. We all know we can't continue polluting the planet – but we still do so. Why?

One reason is humankind's over-reliance on left-brain, cognitive, rational thinking. When we live and think with our heads, we can rationalise anything! Burning down the rainforests, having two cars instead of one, smoking cigarettes – it can all be rationalised away!

Humankind has been described by one famous anthropologist as the enemy of the planet because we live outside the natural rules of the planet. We are against nature. We think up our own rules and act accordingly – and if these do not conform to the external reality of the planet and its own rules, too bad. But we will have to suffer the consequences of our actions, and just as a non-smoker will on average live sixteen years longer than a smoker, we may die in a watery grave as the ice sheets melt and sea levels creep inexorably higher.

Do we have a choice? One way out of this problem is to rely less on traditional, left-brain thinking and develop the holistic, bodily based intelligence discovered by Professor Gendlin and others – to develop our emotional IQ.

How can I develop my emotional intelligence?

1   First realise that there are other forms of intelligence, outside our rational, left-brain IQ – forms of intelligence that may help us live more in harmony with ourselves and our planet
2   Develop that intelligence by learning to focus

A quick guide to learning how to focus

The best way to develop this form of intelligence is to learn it with a trained teacher (details at back of book). Otherwise, here is a quick guide.

NB: Everyone has this innate form of visceral, bodily felt intelligence – the problem is that it has been virtually eradicated by our education system, which puts such an emphasis on left-brain, rational, cognitive thinking.

Those who use this form of emotional intelligence most readily are intuitive people like mothers who are really tuned in to their children's needs; artists and writers, who refer to their non-verbal IQ when completing a work of art; and musicians.

Develop your emotional intelligence by carrying out the following steps:

1   Sit in a quiet place and take any problem you are experiencing currently.

2   Try to identify what this problem does to your body. For example, you were feeling all right before you were suddenly reminded of your problem. Does it give you butterflies in your stomach or a tightening in the throat? What does the problem do to your state of mind? Remember, the word 'disease' means 'lack of ease'. Disease comes from a lack of ease! What does the problem do to your body? What part of your body feels uneasy when you think of it?

3   See if a word, image or picture comes spontaneously to you that identifies the problem. For example, every time you think of your ex-partner you might feel a sharp pain in your left side, just under your heart. Or, when you think of a particular problem in the office, your throat might seize up and you might hardly be able to speak. Stay with this until you are happy that a particular word or image fits. If none comes, just hold on to the feeling of the problem and move on.

4   Take the feeling of the problem and any word or image of it and ask yourself the following question: What is the very worst thing about this problem? Give yourself plenty of time to answer. For example, the worst thing about the problem at work is this: I can't complain about my boss's appalling behaviour because I don't think I'm good enough to get another job.

5   Ask the place deep inside you that is upset the following question: what needs to happen for me to feel all right again? Take your time with this question.

The first temptation will be for you to answer it in your head, with some cliché such as: 'If I think positively, the problem with the boss won't bother me' or 'I'll give the boss an ultimatum – either he changes his attitude or I leave!'

The problem with head-thinking is that it works while you dialogue with yourself, but the moment you take your idea into the real world and confront real relationships, everything can fall apart.

This is where Gendlin's work comes in useful. Gendlin found that if you focus on the painful emotion, it changes. He also discovered that if you keep your focus on the painful emotions, remedies will spontaneously occur to you – remedies that will help you solve the problem and ease the pain. But these will not be 'quick fix' solutions, or ones made up in your head. They will be coming from a place that is far deeper – and when you get the answer and the unease shifts back to ease, you will feel a great sense of relief in the core of your body.

What is this 'shift' of energy like?

Imagine you leave the house and are driving down the road to an important appointment when you suddenly get a feeling that you have left something undone in the house. You rack your brains. Did I lock the door? Yes. Did I put out the cat? Yes. Did I turn off the cooker? Yes. You cannot think of anything else, so you go on driving to your appointment. But the feeling of unease does not go away; instead, it gets worse with every yard you travel further away from home. Finally, the anxiety becomes too much and you pull in, convinced that something is wrong. Your mind urges you to drive on to that urgent appointment but your gut knows different – it knows that something is wrong, and you are wise to listen to it.

You sit for a while focusing on the unease in your body, till your conscious mind finally sees what your unconscious mind was worried about. You left on the heater in the spare room, next to the curtains – a fire could break out at any moment! Quelling your panic, you slam the car into gear and head home, arriving just in time to stop the smouldering curtains from going up in flames.

Now this sort of thing happens all the time, to people everywhere. So what is happening? What part of you knew that something was wrong?

Your conscious mind certainly didn't. It kept urging you to drive on to work and keep your appointment. If you'd listened to your conscious mind, you would have come back to a burnt-out home! So what part of you did know that the heater was left on in the spare room and would burn down the house?

It has many names. In the West we refer to it as the subconscious – the part of consciousness just below the conscious, wakeful state. That is why it can affect and disturb you, like a child crying in a room somewhere at the back of the house. You can hardly hear it with your normal hearing, but a part of you does, and alerts you to the fact that something is wrong. It is the part of you that notes everything and therefore remembers when you have forgotten to do something. It is a deep, visceral part, sometimes referred to as instinct, intuition or gut feeling, and is, as we have seen, ignored at our peril!

This thing has been called many names. Catholics refer to it as conscience. Certain Christians would believe it to be the voice of your guardian angel, whispering a warning to you. Whatever you call it, it works! And without it, we would be the poorer. It knows all the things our conscious minds cannot know at the moment, for the conscious mind has to get you through the day and deal with the hundred and one emergencies that may arise. If it was thinking about something that had happened five weeks or five months ago, let alone five years ago, it would never be able to handle life in the present. That is the function of the subconscious.

In conclusion . . .

As we have seen, the mind/body organism is like a computer's hard drive: it keeps a record of everything that happens. That is why a sudden whiff of perfume can take you back to a memory that is thirty years old! The subconscious remembers everything. The problem is accessing those memories. This is where Gendlin's work comes in very useful, because his focusing technique allows you to access what your subconscious is trying to say to you.

And how will you know that your subconscious is trying to speak to you? You will feel a sense of unease.

Now, if you understand focusing you will be able to listen to that voice of wisdom and conscience, instead of numbing it, distracting yourself from it, denying it or running away from it.

Focusing is one of the great discoveries of the twentieth century. Learn it and you will increase your emotional intelligence many times over.

How can I develop the emotional intelligence of my family?

By doing the following things:

- First, learn to listen to your own internal problems and worries through focusing
- Help your family learn focusing techniques so that they can 'listen' to problems that are bothering them
- Learn total listening, so that you can hear what your family is really saying
- Help your family learn total listening, so that they can hear you!
- Make sure your children know that there are many forms of IQ – not just the sort taught in school
- Look out for the many different ways in which you, your partner and your children are intelligent. Encourage yourself and them to develop these aspects of themselves

Answer the questions on the opposite page (give youself 10 marks for 'Yes' and 0 marks for 'No', or grade yourself somewhere in between these two extremes).

10 9 8 7 6 5 4 3 2 1 0

I am developing my emotional intelligence by, for example, listening to myself and others, expanding the ways I look at life and developing my intuitive intelligence

5

I can be in touch with my own inner feelings, including the painful ones

8

I can express my inner feelings in a nondestructive way, i.e. without the need for alcohol, violence or self-harm

8

I can listen to others unconditionally, without loading them down with my own advice

8

I can tell people at work or at home that they are annoying me – without losing my sense of balance or reason

2

I am finding ways to increase my creativity, for example by writing, going to the theatre or reading

2

I tell my children/partner that there are many types of intelligence and that they are clever and highly inventive in their own way

2

I consider myself to be a uniquely intelligent being – very clever in ways that may not conventionally be thought of as such

9

I listen to my intuition – that small, uneasy feeling in the pit of my stomach – and act on it

2

I express my feelings and do not try to bottle them up

6

Now join up the dots to see a rough guide to your emotional health.

5

100–80	Congratulations! You are in excellent emotional health
79–60	Overall you are emotionally healthy, but some areas need attention
59–50	Borderline. Some areas of your emotional health require immediate attention
49–40	Your overall emotional health is suffering and needs remedial action
39–0	You are emotionally unhealthy. Take action or seek help now to become healthier, or your overall health will suffer!

Step 4
Meeting your Sexual Needs

You are reading this book as a direct result of two people fulfilling their sexual needs. Without sex, you would not be here – it's as simple as that. But whereas every other species on the planet does not seem to have a problem with this reality, we, *Homo sapiens,* have all sorts of difficulties with the subject of sex.

Is the human species not an animal species?

One of the reasons for the problems we have in relation to our sexuality is that we do not actually see ourselves as animals – even though in every way and with every breath we prove our animal origins and existence. We are made up of muscles and sinews, we respire, digest, defecate, and we have a natural life span that ends with us returning to the earth – just like every other carbon-based species. We also, as a species, produce sperm and eggs and need to procreate. Indeed, as biologists have shown, much of our time and energy is spent in pursuit of the propagation of the species.

Fascinating fact: the Internet is all about sex!

A recent survey of Internet usage showed that a large proportion of all hits on the Internet were hits on sex sites.

Also, the vast majority of the billions of pounds spent on Internet products and services goes to sex sites!

This is interesting, for the Internet shows us once again that sex still dominates our time, our thinking and our finances! How? The Internet is a democratic system (so far) and is mainly used by educated people who have the money to access a computer, the skills to operate that computer and the know-how to connect up to a telephone system and an Internet provider. And what are all these sophisticated, intelligent people mainly thinking about and spending their money on? Sex, sex and still more sex!

Sex is still the number one preoccupation for most people on the planet, whether we like it or not. Look at the advertising on our TV screens: much of it is aimed at making us more attractive to a potential mate. Ads for hair products, lipstick, jeans, aftershave, designer clothes are all there to show us at our best, so a would-be mate will be more inclined to accept our sexual advances.

One eminent biologist even declared that the whole of life is sexual, in that it is all geared to continuing itself through the propagation of all its many forms, be they flowers, bees, ants, microbes or even viruses. Every sentient life form is having sex without even stopping to think about it – only man stops and wonders, and deliberates, and then sets rules. And down through history, a large number of *Homo sapiens* have considered sex – the very thing that got them here – as being somehow dirty. But they only feel like this because sex betrays our animal origins like no other activity. We smell, sniff and lick each other in unmentionable places, with parts of our anatomy that we rarely talk about. If our dogs did the same thing on a walk in the park, we would pull them apart from each other, smile awkwardly at the other dog owner and walk quickly in the opposite direction. (I know – I have a dog!) But it's all right for dogs to do that – after all, they're only animals, while we are . . .

Well, according to some members of our species, we are altogether loftier and more divine than dogs. We are a species made in the image of God. But if God made anything, He made sex first, for without it there would be no one around. So we can blame God for the embarrassing positions sex puts us into. No wonder intimate lovers become tongued-tied when their young children demand to know where they came from. It really is so embarrassing.

But the sexual instinct – the one the philosopher Schopenhauer called the 'will to life' – is bigger than any embarrassment, or man-made rule or prohibition. It is the instinct for life itself and will be denied only at our peril. The recent scandals in religious organisations that demand celibacy of their members show just that. The 'will to life' will erupt whatever the prohibition – though often in a twisted and grotesque way, such as in the form of child abuse and paedophilia.

You see, sex is everywhere – all the time. We cannot avoid it. It is the structure of our world – of our universe. The problem is our *attitude* to sex. Fulfilling our sexual needs is as important as filling our stomachs with food and drink – it is a basic life need. Our sexual needs have to be listened to and understood if we are to live happy and contented lives. After all, where does a happy family come from, if not from two consenting adults fulfilling their sexual needs. Without sex, there would be no family, no children, no grandparents, no brothers or sisters. Happy families are sexual families.

So let us now examine the delicate subject of our sexual needs, and how we can fulfil them.

Different types of sexual needs

There are as many different types of sexual needs as there are people on the planet! A man or woman may need to live a life of celibacy in order to feel happy, while another person may need several sexual partners a week to meet their needs. Our Irish Christian culture allows a man one wife, while another culture gives him the luxury (or burden!) of three, four or five wives. How we view our sexuality and our sexual needs depends to a large extent on where and when we were born on the planet.

What are my sexual needs?

First, let us look at the unique 'Irish perspective' on sexuality, for when it comes to sex the Irish have a very particular approach – albeit one that is changing dramatically.

The traditional view of sex in the Republic of Ireland was heavily influenced by the Catholic Church. To paraphrase Frank McCourt's opening to *Angela's Ashes,* there is only one thing more peculiar than an Irish attitude towards sex, and that is a Catholic Irish attitude towards sex!

The Catholic Church had very strongly held views about sex – particularly on when *not* to have it! Sex was for marriage alone. Extramarital sex (including sex on your own) was an occasion for mortal sin and put you on the slippery slope to hell.

What are the results of this particular sort of Irish Catholic upbringing?

In a word, guilt. As we have seen, sex is one of the most powerful forces we experience. Research shows that men have a sexual thought at least once every seven minutes. That's well over 1,000 sexual thoughts a day! This is quite natural. Nature wants us to propagate and must therefore put the need for sex at the forefront of our lives and minds.

So what happens when someone comes along and says: 'Eh! Stop that! No more thoughts on sex.' What does that do to a person? It makes them feel incredibly guilty. As a sexual animal, they cannot stop thinking about sex, so they are doomed to sin.

The Catholic Irish mindset included a certain revulsion towards sex. If sex was so connected to hell and damnation, then it was going to be tarred with the same brush. Because of this, the Catholic Irish mindset was prone to dismiss the very existence of sex. Denial of one's sexuality and sexual needs was the result. But now Ireland is no longer a purely Catholic country, so what has changed in our attitudes?

We are no longer so guilty about sex. Indeed, the younger generations talk openly about it, and it is frankly discussed (some would say ad nauseam!) in the media.

Denial of sex and sexuality has largely disappeared from Irish life, certainly in the younger population. A sign of this is the formal relationship-and-sexuality programme now being taught in all Irish schools; this programme really reflects the change in attitudes in Irish society. Forty years ago, such a programme would have been unimaginable!

Changes in sexual attitudes in Ireland today

There has been a revolution in many Irish attitudes towards the world – not least in relation to sex – in the last few years. As a nation, we have had to change our attitudes towards wealth, immigration, colour prejudice, even the automatic ownership of a house. We have undergone a revolution! In the area of sexuality, we have seen great changes, including:

- The decriminalisation of homosexuality and the emergence of a vibrant gay community, no longer hiding in the shadows
- The uncovering of sexual abuse in the two great bastions of Irish life: the Church and the family
- The open discussion of sexuality, be it on the radio, on TV (especially since the arrival of both satellite and terrestrial television stations from around the world) or in the newspapers

Our attitudes towards sex have changed – and so have our attitudes to each other.

The changing roles of men and women

The traditional roles of men and women in Ireland have changed dramatically in the last few years.

For men

The old certainties are no longer there. Men are no longer the sole breadwinners in most families (and may not even be the biggest earner). They are often no longer the head of the household, while in school and in the workplace they are increasingly being outperformed by women. So dramatic has the change in the status of men been that many psychologists are fearful for the mental health of young males. The education system has recently attempted to respond to this issue by introducing a new programme for boys dealing with the issue of masculinity and its appropriate expression. Suicide rates are climbing. For some, these changes have become too much. In the sexual realm, men are now being confronted by women who demand sexual satisfaction and performance in a way that was unimaginable fifty years ago.

For women

With the advent of contraception, many women are delaying childbearing until their mid-thirties and opting to pursue their careers. The number of single women who own houses is increasing, as is the incidence of single women with high-flying careers. And now over a quarter of all babies born in the Republic are being reared by a single mother. Women are also initiating sexual encounters in a way society never allowed before and are demanding that their sexual needs be meet.

So where does all this leave men?

On the scrap heap, according to some. Or on the emotional dole queue, according to others, waiting to give an odd hand to a busy career women as she dashes from the crèche to her home, via the supermarket. Men are finding themselves in a quandary, no longer the breadwinner, no longer the head of the household, no longer the one who automatically initiates sexual activity. (And with artificial insemination on the increase, they may soon not be needed at all!) So what is happening to man and his sexual needs?

Men's sexual needs

The biological need for man to keep the species going has not slackened during all theses social changes. Man still needs a mate. For one, he needs a receptacle for his sperm: one that will allow him to fertilise an egg and produce a human embryo that will carry his genes on into eternity. But man also requires (or *thinks* he requires) a thing called love!

Sex and love – a recipe for disaster?

Now, it is important to remember that romantic love is a relatively recent invention, perhaps only dating back to the fourteenth century (when it was enjoyed only by the rich and noble). Before then, most sexual needs were met within the bounds of an arranged marriage. This practice continues to the present day in many parts of the world, and statistically it has a much better success rate than romantically inspired marriage.

Why do arranged marriages outlast romantic marriages?

The reasons why arranged marriages survive longer are many and complex. Suitability: arranged marriages take a lot of the risk out of the proceedings. People are matched according to their age, education, social class, intelligence, breeding, family interest, career interests and family traits. The couple will have a lot in common to start off with. There will also be strong family bonds holding the two together when the rough times come along. (It is interesting to note that love does not enter the equation of an arranged marriage at all! But research shows that it often develops as time goes by – and that this sort of love tends to endure.)

Romantic love – the bad news first!

Some behavioural social scientists now believe that romantic love (that intense, obsessive, all-powerful feeling where your lover is everything to you and your happiness depends entirely on their presence) only lasts for around two and a half years. Just long enough, incidentally, for a couple to meet, settle down and conceive!

But all that changed with contraception! Now people can meet, settle down . . . and have no kids for years on end. Some social scientists believe this is not a state nature intended for us. Nature designed us to have children – not to hang around just being in love, which serves no evolutionary need whatsoever! Perhaps the best view of romantic love comes from the philosopher Schopenhauer.

Schopenhauer believed that our basic need, like that of all animals, was to keep the species going. He also observed that what we called love was merely nature's trick to keep us obsessed with one another. (For if we knew the real consequences of being in love, we would never play the game!)

Schopenhauer believed that, in the mating game, we all have little choice but to mate and so we pick the partner that will give us the healthiest offspring (the same criterion all other animals use to select mates). For example, if you have a short, stubby nose, you will tend to pick someone with a long, straight nose. If you are introverted, you will tend to pick an extrovert. (And you would do all this subconsciously). This theory is born out by research in modern genetics and the discovery of the 'selfish gene'.

Schopenhauer also offered some consolation to people who are broken-hearted. Take heart, he told jilted lovers, your former partner only rejected you because you would not have produced the healthiest children. It was really nothing personal!

Now the good news about romantic love!

- It helps us bond and have offspring.
- It is one of the most powerful emotions in the world, causing people to cross continents just to be with their loved one, or kill the loved one if things are not going well. (In France, you can get off a murder charge if you can prove you were in love with the person you killed!)
- It is very good for one's health, causing all the physiological systems to work at their peak. You can even identify people who are in love – they have a certain glow!
- It has inspired some of the greatest stories, love songs, films, poems and works of art.

- It provides the key story content for most of the world's greatest soap operas, films and gossip columns, as well as gossip at work. Without it, we would be bored and have not so much to talk about!

Now we have examined sex and looked at sexuality in general. But we are all individuals, so now is the time to find out what our individual sexual needs are.

Finding out what my sexual needs are

As a result of past religious and social practices in Ireland, many of us are confused about our sexual needs. For some, the question may seem irrelevant and irreverent. Sexual needs . . . I don't have them! But as every book from the Bible to the writings of Freud says: we were born to fall in love, procreate and have offspring. And that means having sex!

An exercise to help you discover your sexual needs

Take a quiet moment to close your eyes and imagine the following: you are about to have your ideal sexual encounter – one that will meet all your current needs. Take all the time in the world. Make notes if it helps – but if you do, don't leave the notes lying around!

Where would I be when I have all my sexual needs meet?

Who would I be with?

What things would I be doing to my partner?

What things would they be doing to me?

How long would this go on for?

You might also like to examine the sexual thoughts and fantasies that you have forbidden yourself. This is unlikely to make them any more troublesome, for there is ample evidence to show that suppressing emotions, yearnings and needs only makes them stronger. Also, sex is all about imagination. What kills sex in marriage and long-term relationships is boredom, so if you want to be a happy lover with one partner for a long time, start letting your imagination run riot. (Remember: you do not have to act on your imaginings. Just allow yourself the luxury of seeing what they are!)

What does my imagination teach me about my sexual needs, when I set it free?

1

2

3

How can I go about fulfilling my desires?

Step 1

Step 2

Step 3

If you have problems discovering – or accepting – your sexuality or sexual needs, seek professional advice. You can start with your GP, who will be able to put you in touch with expert help. (Remember, your sexuality is one of the easiest things to corrupt or destroy when you are young. But help is at hand – you only have to reach out for it.)

Are my sexual needs being met?

Answer the following questions as truthfully as possible:

Am I happy with the sexual content of my life?

Am I getting enough sexual activity?

Am I with the right sexual partner?

If the answer to any of the above is 'No', then you have a problem. (Remember, having no sexual activity may also be the 'right' answer for you.)

Here are some tips to follow if your sexual needs are not being met.

I am in a long-term relationship and my needs are not being met

Talk about it with your partner. Communication is everything. If you are not having a good time sexually, then your partner probably isn't either.

If you cannot talk about it – or it ends up in a row – seek help. Many couples in long-term relationships have problems. For instance, children arrive and things change dramatically, with no sleep and anxious nights for the new parents. Or there is death in the family, or illness, or financial strain. Then sex is the first thing to go. But there is a remedy out there, in the form of professional help. Start with a visit to your GP. He or she will ensure you get to see the right therapist.

But it will take effort. People get stuck in a rut and things become uncomfortably comfortable. But remember the old saying: What is the difference between being in a rut and being six foot under? About five foot.

If you are stuck in a sexual rut with your partner and are short of ideas, you can buy things that will stimulate your sex life. There are ample videos and books on how to improve the quality of your sex life – all it requires is the effort to go out there and buy them. The problem is that we become complacent. Sometimes we choose to take the easy option. Some married couples let the sexual part of their marriage wither and die. This is not a good idea. As we have seen, we are all sexual beings, and sex is the oxygen that helps keep long-term relationships alive. Let the sex die, and the relationship may starve to death. What may happen then is that one of partner may meet someone who gets their sexual juices flowing again – and that can spell disaster. Be wise, and put the effort in before it comes to that.

How sexual energy waxes and wanes during a relationship

Sex, like everything else, changes during a relationship. Kids come along, and a couple's energy goes into them rather than each other. This is natural and normal for a time, but it is dangerous to let it continue for too long. Also, as we get older our need for sexual activity declines. Again, this is natural and normal. I know several couples who have taken the French philosopher Montaigne's advice and become best friends. Sex, in this context, is not an issue. The problem is when outside influences interfere with the couple's sexual activity (or lack of it).

Sex and the Celtic Tiger

It often seems that the Celtic tiger is devouring the sexual appetites of many Irish men and women.

Men come home from work wrecked. They have spent the whole day in a high-pressure job and have endured terrific stress – and this is not made any better by sitting in a traffic jam for two hours in the evening. It is hardly surprising that these men do not want to climb into bed and jump all over their partners as soon as they get home.

Women may find the going even tougher. Not only do they have to work, they also often have to do the shopping and raise the kids. For the latest research shows that the 'new man' is largely a myth. Women still do most of the housework, while at the same time holding down a full-time job and raising the kids. With all this on their plate, they do not have the energy for passionate lovemaking!

Now we know that these demands are not good for sexual relationships, and for many couples the warning bells are ringing. If they want to stop the drift, they have to arrange a time to make love. Try scheduling it in, like a golf outing! I know this sounds artificial, but sometimes one has to be this calculating, otherwise a fracture can develop between partners – and eventually split them asunder.

Worrying statistics on marital break-up

Ireland is fast catching up on the USA and the UK in terms of the incidence of marital break-up. In the USA and the UK, up to half of all marriages end in divorce – and this figure does not include the separations, both physical and emotional, that take place in other long-term relationships.

Separation is divorce by another name, for many couples now cannot afford to live in separate households and have to put up with leading separate lives under the same roof. In many ways, this is worse than divorce: with warring couples forced to stay together, the war inevitably gets worse.

Improve your chances of staying together

Overall, the chances of a long-term relationship working out are around 1 in 3. While a third of all long-term relationships flourish, the other two-thirds end in either a formal divorce or an informal split. If you want to give your long term marriage or relationship a chance, you have to put great effort into it. Part of that effort is to keep the sexual relationship healthy.

Sex is no cure-all

But sex is not a cure-all. It will not hold a fractured or abusive relationship together for long. What it may do is keep a fifty-fifty relationship limping along, and nourish a healthy, ongoing relationship. Sex is the glue of intimate relationships and ignoring it is risky. If you want to have a happy family, you are going to need to have a happy sex life – so get out there and practice!

Recap of main points on having a healthy sex life

- Know what you want sexually
- Learn to listen closely to your partner
- Put in the necessary time and effort to make love to your partner – set aside time, buy a video, buy some massage oil and a scented candle, put the kids to bed early, have a glass of wine and get to it!
- Seek professional advice if you are having serious problems or difficulties – don't let it slide. Start with your GP: he or she will put you on the right track

What if I am single again and looking for a partner?

If you were previously in a serious relationship and now find yourself single again but want to start over, here are some tips:

- Draw up a plan and give yourself deadlines to find a partner. Force yourself to follow that plan and go out more.
- Don't fixate on the outcome – concentrate instead on the process of getting out to meet new people. Let fate decide the outcome.
- Change your appearance. Treat yourself to new clothes, a new haircut or a make-over, and you will feel more confident. Successful dating is all about confidence.
- Tone up your body – go to the gym. When you eventually do meet a new partner, you will have pride and confidence in your body!
- Take up a hobby. It will sharpen up your interest in

life, give you things to talk about and help you meet new people.

- Don't be afraid to try reputable dating agencies. Nowadays, with people working unsociable hours, a good dating agency is a serious option for busy people.

Set yourself goals and work at them and you will be surprised what the result is! But again, don't fixate on the outcome – let it happen. Leave who you meet, and how it progresses, in the hands of Cupid! Remember, fulfilling your healthy sexual needs (i.e. those that do not involve abusing yourself or others) will make you physically and emotionally healthier. Sex is at the core of our being and rewards us if we attend to its needs. But finding fulfilment of our sexual needs is only one part of being well. We need more than sex to be fulfilled, which brings us to our next step: filling our lives with a variety of healthy relationships.

Step 5
Finding and Developing
Healthy Relationships

We are not islands. We need interaction. We need stimulation. We need other people! And we need them in every part of our lives.

One of the problems with romantic love is the idea that all our relationship needs will be met by one person. This is obviously impossible. It puts an unbearable strain on the 'one' person, and the expectation that one person can meet all your needs may break the relationship.

It is also a tacky idea, for when people fall in love in this romantic and exclusive way, they tend suddenly and mysteriously to disappear from other people's lives. The daily phone calls end. The weekly meetings cease. It's as if they had died! Weeks later, you find them wrapped around the new love of their life in the corner of the pub. They tell you they have found true happiness at last. After promising to be back in touch, they forget to phone for weeks.

If the person is a really good friend of yours, you may forgive them this aberration and keep in contact when the torrid affair ends – as it invariably will. For no one can bear the strain of that intensity. Instead, it burns up gloriously and quickly, like a shooting star. You see, no one can meet all of another person's needs, however much they love them. That sort of totally dependent relationship happens just once in each lifetime – with our mother, when we are squealing infants! And then nature gives us about two years to grow out of it – literally!

That is why romantic, obsessive love is regarded as

infantile by psychologists, who describe it as a regression into babyhood! Even the lover's vocabulary betrays infantile aspects: the object of affection becomes 'my baby', and lovers coo and fondle each other as they would an infant.

This is all very well while it lasts – but it rarely does. Meanwhile, the lover has lost contact with all his or her old friends and has to go cap in hand to them when the relationship ends. Of course, we all need that special one-on-one love relationship, but we also need a whole other gamut of relationships if we are to flourish and grow as human beings, both inside and outside a family. Happy families are friendly families, who are connected to a whole range of people. We need many people in our lives if we are to remain stimulated and challenged. Let's now check just how healthy your relationships are and how many kinds of relationships you have.

Questionnaire: Are my relationships both inside and outside my relationship varied and healthy?

On the chart on the next page, give yourself 10 marks for 'Yes', 0 marks for 'No', or grade yourself somewhere between the two.

	Yes									No	
	10	9	8	7	6	5	4	3	2	1	0

I have close relationships outside my immediate family/spouse relationship, e.g. with friends, colleagues and neighbours — 1

I keep in touch with my old friends — 1

I keep in touch with memebers of my wider family circle, e.g. aunts, cousins — 1

I have hobbies and interests that keep me connected to people outside my immediate family — 0

I keep my love relationship fresh and interesting — 5

If I have arguments with my partner, I take effective steps to heal them — 10

I sacrifice my personal goals, like golf, sport and time alone, when my children or partner needs me to — 10

I compromise and share when my family or partner needs me to — 10

I remain committed to my family or partner even when I feel like ending the relationship — 10

I do not verbally or physically abuse my partner or family — 10

/ 57

100–80	I have many happy and varied relationships in my life – and am happy with them!
79–60	Overall, I have good, varied relationships, though I could work more on some of them
59–40	My relationships in some areas are good but in other areas need urgent attention
30–0	I need to take a serious look at the quality and number of my relationships

What sort of relationships do I need?

We need many kinds of relationships: here are just some of them. Tick off the ones you are currently enjoying:

- Close Romantic love or sexual relationships
- Close family relationships
    mother and father
    sons and daughters
    brothers and sisters
    aunts and uncles
    cousins, nephews and nieces
- Friends from:
    childhood
    school
    college
    sporting activities
    hobbies and interests
    work

- Colleagues from
    work
    professional organisations
    voluntary organisations
    church
- Neighbours

They say that you can number your real friends on one hand – we do not have the time to have more than four or five close friends. But our lives can still be filled with a variety of people who add to our lives in some way. Let us now carry out an audit of how many relationships we have in our lives – and the quality of those relationships.

Number and quality of relationships in my life

Give 10 points for an excellent relationship and 0 for a non-existent or poor relationship.

	Type of relationship	Score
1	Close romantic love or sexual relationships	☐ 10
2	Close family relationships:	
	mother and father	☐ 0
	sons or daughters	☐ 10
	brothers and sisters	☐ 6
	aunts and uncles	☐ 0
	cousins, nephews and nieces	☐ 6

3   Friends from:
         childhood   ☐ 2
         school   ☐ 2
         college   ☐ 0
         sporting activities   ☐ 0
         hobbies and interests ☐ 0
         work   ☐ 0

4   Colleagues from:

         work   ☐ 0
         professional organisations ☐ 0
         voluntary organisations   ☐ 0
         church   ☐ 0

5   Neighbours   ☐ 2

Check each score against the appropriate category:

10-8   A really satisfying relationship – cherish it
             and do not let it go!
7-6   A good relationship that could perhaps be
             deepened
5-4   This relationship definitely needs work if
             it is to flourish
3 and below A relationship that is non-existent or does
             not work in any real sense

Now go down the list again and ask yourself the following questions:

Which areas in my life are deficient in relationships?

How do I not give enough of myself in these relationships?

What could I do to deepen or extend these relationships?

Steps we can take to improve relationships

Relationships need attention

Attention is the key ingredient in any relationship. Without attention, the relationship – be it with a pet, plant or boyfriend – will die. You can tell a child you love them, but if you are constantly away at work and give them no attention they will not really believe you. You may buy them fancy presents to make up for your lack of attention, but they will simply see through this. Children need attention. Attention is love. Adults also need attention. Pets need attention. Even plants need attention. And attention needs one thing in order to function: time!

Relationships need time

You cannot give someone your attention if you do not have time to do so. But time is a rare commodity these days, with the Celtic Tiger gobbling up every available second.

Couples, kids and teenagers hardly have time for themselves, let alone for others. If you want a relationship to succeed, you have to make time in a very crowded schedule, otherwise the relationship will die.

For example, children nowadays are being reared by parents they rarely see. This is especially the case with fathers, who often leave the house early and arrive back late and exhausted. What will a boy think if his dad is often absent, misses his football matches at school and tries to make up for all this by buying him presents? It does not work: the child will feel only resentment. The same can be said of a husband and wife. Time is the essential ingredient in any relationship; without it, the relationship will wither and die.

How do I make time for my relationships?

Schedule time in your diary in the same as you would a business meeting – it is the only way to ensure you turn up. Make the time 'quality time'. It is better to be with your child for an hour of your undivided attention rather than to be with him for three hours while answering your mobile phone every few minutes. You could end up having a worse time than if you had not turned up at all. Quality time impresses on the child that they are important to you.

Relationships demand compromise

Another of the great fallacies of romantic love is that it is effortless. You turn up like Bruce Willis, your true love falls into your muscular arms and you whisk her away to a life of eternal happiness. There is no effort involved: you are in love, and that is enough. Happiness will flow naturally from such a union and you will both be totally fulfilled. The drug of love will keep you happy forever!

Unfortunately, nothing could be further from the truth, as anyone who has had a relationship will attest! Let us look at some of the reasons why this is so.

The hierarchy of needs

The social scientist Abraham Maslow understood that human beings have a hierarchy of needs. We need certain things if we are to live fulfilled lives. Adapted to the Irish context, we can look at Maslow's hierarchy in the following way.

First, we need food, shelter and security from a hostile world. Without these things, we cannot proceed to the next level. (Unfortunately, many people in the world do not have these basic requirements and spend their lives in misery, hovering on the verge of death. Anyone living in Ireland 150 years ago had the very same experience.)

Secondly, we need medical assistance, sanitation, reliable food production and fuel. Without these, we cannot go on to the next level. Thirdly, we need medical care, education, and gainful employment. Without these we cannot go on to the next level. Fourthly, we need the resources (money and leisure) to give ourselves the time to decide what to do with our lives. Now we are reaching the top of the pyramid, where we can 'self-actualise', to use Maslow's words.

At the top of the pyramid, we reflect on life and decide what we are going to do with our lives. This is a privileged position that few people in the world enjoy. Most people in the world are worrying whether they will eat today: we in Ireland are worrying about what we will eat today. In the same way, we have the luxury of deciding what we will do with our lives. This is what Maslow called self-actualisation: you and I have the privilege of going out and choosing our destiny today. We should cherish and respect the fact that we are in this position.

The downside of being in a position to self-actualise: self-obsession!

The problem with being able to self-actualise is that it can make an individual self-aware to the point of self-obsession. We get used to:

- fulfilling our own needs
- pursuing our own careers
- going on our own holidays
- pleasing ourselves

The advertisements on television proclaim the ego message in a nutshell: I do this 'Because I'm worth it!' But what happens when two people with this attitude meet and form a relationship that ultimately produces children?

There is an immediate conflict of self-interest. Two individuals who have been used to pleasing themselves suddenly face demands on their time, money and patience. They can no longer do what they want. They can no longer pursue the life of their dreams. The man suddenly has a pregnant wife, who may want to give up her job to rear the baby. Bang goes the second holiday and the subscription to the golf club.

The woman suddenly has a conflict of needs. She wants desperately to care for her baby, but that will mean jeopardising her position at work. She is being torn apart and getting little help, for her husband is no longer the charming lover of their courting days but a tired and irritable man, showing signs of petulance as a result of being deprived of his sleep.

Change some of the details of our story and you have the picture of many Irish marriages today. There is an inherent conflict between the 'I'm worth it!' generation and the hard, tedious grind that fills much of long-term relationships and child-rearing.

And research shows that people are not being educated – and therefore not being prepared – for the demands of long-term relationships and child-rearing. Their preparation is how Chandler gets on with Monica in *Friends,* or how Posh Spice gets on with Becks in *Hello* magazine – all fairy-tale stuff, but no more real or relevant to our lives than an Australian soap opera. Perhaps this appalling lack of real education around relationships is the reason why two-thirds of all relationships run into serious difficulties, and why up to half end in divorce. We are living with the consequences of an education system focused solely on points, while ignoring the need to educate for living.

So what do long-term child-rearing relationships demand?

Compromise of your personal needs. The two annual holidays, the second car, the weekend trips away: all may have to go when a child arrives. Also, personal goals – like going back into full-time education or learning a new skill – may have to be put on hold if the new three-way relationship is to succeed.

Self-sacrifice. Some of our needs must be put second, so that the relationship and family can survive and thrive.

But self-sacrifice is difficult for a generation raised in a culture where people do what they want, because they're worth it! Self-sacrifice is not particularly romantic or sexy, so it is not particularly popular. But if a child-rearing relationship is to work, self-sacrifice, at one level or another – be it time, sleep or recreation – is going to have to take place.

The need for commitment. In modern Ireland, we have witnessed a revolution in the workplace. Twenty years ago, you were considered lucky to have a job. Nowadays, people are being imported into the country to fill jobs Irish people will not do! Suddenly, rather than being happy to have a job, people are being very choosy, and if the boss looks at them strangely or makes 'unnecessary' demands, they up and leave at the drop of a hat. Something similar is happening in relationships. People have very high expectations of relationships, usually based on the false premise that the feeling of love will last forever.

But experience and statistics show that the honeymoon period eventually ends and the trials begin. She suddenly finds his habit of leaving his smelly socks at the top of the stairs for washing no longer acceptable. He suddenly finds her PMT mood swings not so understandable, stops making allowances for them and starts shouting back. Anger outbursts are followed by sullen periods of silence. The couple do not make love for a week. He starts staying out late; she stops making his meals and cleaning up after him. Reality hits home. Both start to think the whole thing is not worth it. They never had this hassle when they were single: do they need it now? Both secretly start wondering what it would be like if they were single again.

Now is the moment of critical choice: will they stay together or not? But it is difficult, because both individuals are used to getting their own way and calling the shots. If she had been spoken to in the workplace in the same way her husband speaks to her, she would have had her boss in the labour court immediately. If he had been treated in a management meeting in the same way his wife treats him, he would have walked straight over to his solicitor and taken a case against the firm. But this is not the office, this is not a management meeting – this is a marriage, and there could be a child on the way. Can he walk out? Can she pack up her bag, start divorce proceedings and move back into her mum's until the house is sold?

The answer to both questions is 'Yes'. Both can walk out – and, increasingly, they do. Very many Irish marriages break down irretrievably, even when the couple do not divorce. They simply start leading separate lives under the same roof. If we are not careful, people will soon start to split up or divorce each other because the marriage has become inconvenient. It is here that commitment counts, and where vows taken or promises made are honoured. It does not mean an abusive relationship must be tolerated – quite the opposite. But the idea that we can leave a love partner or spouse simply because things are not working out is becoming so commonplace as to be ridiculous. Commitment can and does work, but the real test is: does it work when things gets tough – as they always do?

Step 6
Finding rewarding work and exercising your personal power

There are two key questions that must be asked about work and the happy family:

* Is the work I am doing the work I want to do?
* Is there a reasonable balance between my family life and my work life, or is one dominating and damaging the other?

Questionnaire: Is my work life balanced and happy?

On the chart opposite, give yourself 10 marks if you agree with the statement completely, 0 if you disagree completely, or give yourself a score somewhere between the two.

I am very happy in the work I do   5

I do not come home from work
    stressed out   6

My partner is happy with my work and
    the way I handle it   7

My children are happy with the time my
    work allows me to spend with them   10

I can leave work at the agreed time
    and spend weekends and holidays
    with my family   10

My work is not stressing me to death or
    affecting my health   4

If I had the chance to change my
    career, I would still be doing what I
    am now   2

My job gives me plenty of opportunities
    to progress up the career ladder   0

My job allows me to continue my
    education   0

My job is creative and allows me to
    express myself and my personal
    power   2
                                                                        _____

                                                                          46

100–80 You are very happy in your chosen career
79–70 You are happy enough in your chosen career, apart from a few aspects of it
69–50 You are getting by, but you need changes to your career and your balance between work and home
49–40 You are not happy with your job and how it affects your family life
39–0 Your job is jeopardising your health and making your family life unhappy

Is the work I am doing what I really want to do?

It is difficult to be happy in your family life if you are not happy with your job. Unfortunately, if you are unhappy with your job, making changes will require courage and effort. It may also involve considerable risk.

'I've a mortgage – I can't afford to change my job,' you may say, or 'I've young kids, I can't put their future at stake.' But the truth is that many individuals change their careers mid-life and do so successfully.

Fascinating facts

Q: What do Anita Roddick, the painter Gauguin and President George W. Bush all have in common?
A: All changed careers mid-life.

Anita Roddick was a housewife and mother when she started making and selling natural cosmetic products in her kitchen in Brighton. Gauguin was a bank manager when, at the age of forty-five, he gave up everything for his first love: painting. George W. Bush was basically unemployed in his thirties and drifting. He was also suffering from alcoholism. Then he became involved in running a baseball team and seemed to have found his niche – he made the team a great success. Then in 1994 he shocked his friends by announcing he was giving up his career as a baseball-club owner and going into politics - something nobody thought he would do well at.

The results of these midlife career changes were as follows:

- Anita Roddick went on to found the Body Shop and become a billionaire
- Gauguin became one of the most recognised painters of all time
- George W. Bush became the forty-third president of the United States just six years years after changing his career and entering politics.

Lesson: It is never too late to change your career successfully. You just need what the above people had:

- the courage to make the change
- an ability to take big risks with your future and that of your family
- patience
- determination

Then, surprisingly, a large dose of luck usually comes along when these things have been done!

If you want to find out what you really want to do in life, complete the exercise on the opposite page.

Your ideal career

Below, draw a picture of yourself pursuing the career you would like to do if you were guaranteed success and were not worried about money. Make the picture as detailed as possible, and describe under it the nature of your dream job. Writing and drawing uses both sides of your brain!

The advantages of pursuing the career of your choice are that you will:

- get up earlier and work longer hours without complaint
- be more motivated
- be more enthusiastic ('enthusiasm' means 'being filled with God')

As a result of all this, you will be more successful at what you do. You will also be healthier and live longer!

The Irish lady and the Italian job

I know the lady who owns the best coffee shop in Dublin. When she was young, she went to Italy to study art and married an Italian. Years later she returned, and together they opened a small shop selling Italian food and wine. They had a small area in the shop where people could sit and sample the goods. They only sold the very finest Italian produce and charged very modest rates. When I first went in to have a coffee, the lady had to think of the price and only charged me a pound. (The usual price for a cup of coffee in Dublin at the time was about £1.50.) When I told her she should increase her prices she said she was not interested in making money, she just loved serving fine Italian food and making her customers happy.

The shop was run by the lady and her family. They would prepare each antipasta dish by hand, toasting the ciabiatta, pouring on the olive oil and rubbing in fresh garlic. It was mouth-watering. When I first started going to the shop, it was not too busy. But gradually I noticed the magic which comes from doing what you love taking its effect. Within months the place was buzzing, and by the first Christmas

How Important is freedom
To You?

you could not get a seat in the shop. They had also started selling gift hampers filled with Italian wine, cheese and meats. Soon they were so busy with orders that they had to work late into the night. One local company ordered sixty hampers as gifts for their clients!

An idea that had started as a hobby of sorts had become a spectacular success, and as I sat sipping my espresso one morning, it came to me that their success was based on three things:

- love of what they were doing
- lack of regard for financial success
- purity of intent in the way they insisted on using only the finest products

I asked the lady if I could include her story in this book and she agreed, sitting down and telling me a little more of her history. She had gone to Rome to study art and had met the man of her dreams and settled down. They both had excellent jobs, he in an Italian government ministry and she in the UN (with a tax-free salary!). But both were bored and missed being with their young children during the day, so they decided to return to Ireland and set up shop – literally! This involved a tremendous risk. They would both have to give up pensioned, secure and, in her case, tax-free jobs. But they decided it was worth the risk. Their first venture, a corner shop, turned out not to be their cup of tea, but they stuck at it and started to bring in Italian wines and cheeses, which sold well. They then set up a wholesale outlet. This is where the sofa and the few tables and chairs came in, scattered around the shop, turning it into a living room.

People started to sample the goods and soon they had a steady trade, but because Eileen and Stefano kept putting in the hours and attending to their customers themselves, the trade grew. At Christmas I saw a senior Cabinet minister, an editor of a Sunday newspaper and a top journalist all sampling the antipasti, and this brought about my one and only complaint about the shop: they were becoming too popular!

Eileen puts their success down to the following factors:

- caring about their customers
- not worrying about making a profit
- bringing in only the very best produce
- making sure that herself, her husband and her family members serve regularly in the shop

They now have three outlets and are expanding. The only problem they face now is how to keep the business personal.

Whenever I give talks or write about changing career mid-life, I always get the same complaint: 'We've a mortgage', 'We've kids', 'We can't take the risk', 'We'd be acting irresponsibly', or 'It's all right for you to speak like that – you're a writer' (whatever that means!). People talk themselves out of their dreams just as quickly as they dream them. It is possible to make career changes if you are prepared to take the risk and follow your heart. If you are not prepared to do that then, as the Americans say, drop the idea, get off the pot and get on with what you already have! Complaining for no purpose is a less-than-useless task.

If, on the other hand, you find you really want to make a career change, here are a few ideas.

What can I do if I find I am working in the wrong job?

Reflect. Changing careers involves a process of exploring your current interests, aptitudes, skills and personality, and matching them with opportunities available in the economy, just like my Italian friend did.

My coauthor, Brian Mooney, deals with people in this situation on an ongoing basis, and he suggests that someone who is seriously considering a career change should visit a career-guidance counselling service as a first step.

There are a number of excellent interest inventories which counsellors can use as an initial exploration of career interest. You would be amazed at what such a process can generate. After this, taking a set of aptitude tests will provide an insight into the skill base of the person; this can then be matched with the results of the exploration of current interests. Whether one has the personality traits suitable for a particular career can be explored through a range of personality tests.

Having come to a determination as to what new career areas are worth pursuing, the person needs to compile an up-to-date CV, which may need to be adapted to the particular job being sought.

Once you have an idea of an alternative career, take time out to research it. Find out:

- whether there is a market locally and globally for what you are thinking of doing
- whether there are training schemes. For example, FÁS and other government-run schemes pay you to retrain!
- whether there are start-up grants and tax incentives available

150

Do you have resources you can put into any new venture, for example by remortgaging your house or taking out a bank loan or overdraft?

Draw up a business plan. Find a friendly accountant and go through the figures. (This is a very important step.) Talk to your solicitor and ask his advice. Visit your doctor and check that your health is up to what you plan to do. Get plenty of feedback before you make your decision – but do not necessarily be put off by it. (Professional people are not necessarily good at taking risks: they tend to be more conservative and give advice accordingly. In the story of the Italian café, Eileen was advised by an accountant not to open her Italian shop – he looked at the figures she gave him and was convinced she would not make money!)

Find someone who is already doing what you are proposing to do and write, e-mail or talk to them. Don't be shy. In my experience, people who have made it in one career are usually willing to share their experiences – and hearing about these experiences can be invaluable.

Finally, when you have done all of the above, *go away and find a quiet place,* like a church or a mountainside, and ask for guidance from the universe (or whatever you regard as the higher power). And I tell you this: you will get an answer right in the core of your gut! Remember: you are important, and what you do counts. If you take a risk and go for something new, something which is meant for you, you will get help! The universe needs people to be functioning at their best. It also needs people to be happy in what they do. Happiness is merely the end result of things going well in your life. If you are doing something you hate, your unhappiness will spread to everyone else in your life: your family, friends and work colleagues.

Remember, you are unique. Mother Theresa of Calcutta told Bob Geldof when he was organising Live Aid that 'There is something in the world that only you can do and something only I can do.' This applies to everyone on the planet. The trick is finding the thing that you can do. If you do find it and pursue it with courage, the universe will do the rest. Good luck on your quest!

Now whether you are in the right job or the wrong job, you can still be unbalanced in the time you spend on it. If you have a family, you have commitments. So now let us check:

Is there a reasonable balance between my family life and work life?

The claws of the Celtic Tiger

Tigers are dangerous animals. In the wild they pose little threat to people, but let them out on the streets of a city and they will turn on you and rip you to pieces. This is what has happened with the Celtic Tiger in Ireland. While we were riding on its back, we were taken on a great ride to places that we had not seen before. Riches, dreams, holidays and a car of our choice were all there for the taking. But as the Celtic Tiger leaped over the prosperity fence, many of the people who were riding the tiger's back fell off. The Celtic Tiger then turned on them and is beginning to devour them, bit by bit. Tigers – Celtic or otherwise – are dangerous. Never forget that!

So how is the Celtic
Tiger devouring us?

The Celtic Tiger is devouring our time. As corporate America expands in Ireland, the culture of get-in-early-and-leave-late is taking hold. Recent figures show that Irish people are working far longer hours than before. People arrive at work earlier to avoid the traffic and leave later. They are also being asked to work weekends. This applies even to people who are paid to work only to 5.30 pm: because of the culture of fear, they will not leave the office before the boss. This of course means rows at home, when they arrive late. The Celtic Tiger is devouring our time – and your time.

The Celtic Tiger is devouring our good nature. Year ago, if you pulled out in front of an oncoming car, you would get a blast of a horn and a good curse. Now you might get a fist through your windscreen! Road rage is just one symptom of the way the Irish are losing their cool as the economy hots up. Irish civility, hospitality and plain good *craic* are being devoured by the avaricious Celtic Tiger. We are becoming more and more like some of our American neighbours – rude, short-tempered and crabby.

The Celtic Tiger is devouring our patience. When I arrived in Dublin from London twenty years ago, I was amazed at just how relaxed people were. I used to think this was a shortcoming, but now, seeing the increasing American-isation of Irish working practices, I am not so sure. Before, people were patient with strangers: they stopped in the street and gave directions, often striking up a conversation. Nowadays, all that has changed. Now if people stop, it is often to give directions with a long face. Some seem offended that yet another 'foreigner' has taken up their time. We are losing our patience and racism has reared its ugly head. The Celtic Tiger is really starting to maul the Irish soul. What will be left when it has finished is anybody's guess.

What can I do if work takes me away from my family for longer than I should be away from them?

Check to see if you are away too long from your home, partner and children by answering the following questions:

	Yes	No
I feel my work comes before my family	☑	☐
My partner and/or children feel my work comes before them	☐	☑
My work colleagues think I work too much	☐	☑
My children are sometimes left on their own/ come back to an empty house/ have to cook their own meals/ don't see me at their sports day or matches	☐	☑
I am tired/exhausted/anxious/irritable when I get home from work	☑	☐
I often work past the time I am contracted to	☐	☑
I find I am increasingly working weekends	☐	☑
I feel my health is suffering because of my work	☑	☐

If you answered 'Yes' to more than three of the above, you are working at the expense of your family life. The consequences of this are appalling, and include:

- ill-health (even premature death) through stress-related illness
- marital disharmony and break-up
- long-term resentment from your children
- increase in alcoholism and addictions, to block out stress
- emotional ill health, breakdown and an increase in depression
- increased absenteeism

What we fear usually gets us in the end, if we do not face it. In this case, the marauding Celtic Tiger, in the form of an over-demanding boss or job, must be faced head-on if you and your family are to survive. Kowtowing to an over-demanding boss can be fatal in the long term.

So what can I do if I am being taken advantage of in my job?

'I have a mortgage.'
'I have children with expensive tastes.'
'I have two cars to run and holidays to pay for.'
'I am up to my eyes in debt.'
'Please tell me: what can I do?'

The answer to these increasingly common problems is not easy, but this much is true: you have two choices. Either:

- suffer the consequences of your current job or career or
- change your current job or career

The trouble is that changing your career will require:

- discipline
- courage
- endurance

But take heart: dozens of people change their careers every day in Ireland – many successfully. If you are considering changing career, it is important that you:

- fully understand the consequences of *not* changing
- think of yourself as taking 'the Hero's Journey'

'The Hero's Journey': how the universe helps those who risk all!

Joseph Campbell, the great mythologist who died in the 1990s, spent his life studying the great storytellers, from the people who made the first cave paintings, to the Greeks and Romans, to the aborigines of Australia and the Native American Indians, right down to storytellers of the present day. He also examined the stories and wisdom of all the great religions – Christianity, Islam, Buddhism, Hinduism and Judaism – and reached the following conclusion: that each person embarks on a journey to discover their own unique destiny, be it marriage, motherhood, a job, artistic endeavour or being a warrior. But every journey – whether you are a milkman or the prime minister – is hard and filled with pitfalls, shadows and enemies. You can be ambushed on your journey. You can also sit at home and refuse to take the journey. But if you show the courage and determination to take the journey, you will meet with unexpected help on the way, in the form of mentors, supernatural help, grace, coincidence and serendipity! The one thing that is needed above all for you to succeed on the journey and discover your true destiny is this: you must risk all you have at some point on the journey.

One of the greatest fans of Joseph Campbell was George Lucas: the idea of 'the Hero's Journey' inspired Lucas's film *Star Wars.* The director's interest in Campbell helps explain the phenomenal appeal of *Star Wars:* it touches on universal themes and needs – things we all intuitively understand. My next book is about the Hero's Journey and guides you through its various stages. (Details of this book and Kevin Flanagan's other books can be found at the back of this book.)

Here are the key steps of the Hero's Journey, to help you find your destiny and overcome the obstacles in your life. (The word 'hero' is used here to refer to both men and women.)

The steps of the hero's journey

- The ordinary world, where all is well
- A crisis develops, its shadow casting a pall on the horizon
- The hero gets a call to action – a way to deal with the crisis
- The hero refuses the call to action through fear
- A mentor arrives to give the hero advice, or supernatural help intervenes
- The hero now accepts the call to action and begins the journey
- The hero's journey consists of a road of trials, where the hero is ambushed by his or her greatest terrors (real or imagined), bogged down by his or her doubts and paralysed by his or her fears. These fears can be psychological fears inside the hero, or real fears in the form of enemies and traitors. Please note: at any point,

the hero can be defeated by his fears, and return home beaten. Sometimes he will not make it home but will die in the wilderness, a lost soul.

- On the road of trials, the hero often finds that they take three steps forward but two back. The hero often faces defeat or disillusionment but always gets help from the mentor, or supernatural help intervenes. They complete the road of trials and face the final battle – the battle with their innermost fear or greatest enemy – or both!
- The hero must risk all to win the final battle, but the battle appears to go against him, and all is lost
- Supernatural help arrives at the very last moment and the hero makes one last dying act of defiance
- Against hope and against all the odds, the hero wins and, through winning, is changed. No longer unsure, the hero returns home a changed person, bringing back the prize of the journey: the rich elixir of experience
- The hero shares the rich elixir of experience with his family and tribe and they learn from him. Now they can in turn become mentors to their family and friends or to strangers as they go on their own hero's journey
- The hero now knows the secret to success: that you must risk all if you are to succeed! And the only way the hero could discover this secret was by completing the journey for themselves

Risking all in making change

The real lesson of the Hero's Journey is that, if you want to make changes in your life, you must risk everything. It is no use going about things half-heartedly. If you do decide to make a change in your home life or work practice, do it with all your heart and risk everything: you are unlikely to be disappointed!

Exerting your personal power

Exerting personal power entails:

- making decisions
- taking risks
- confronting your enemies – both inside and outside yourself
- going into battle alone – but finding help once you are there

Go on: risk everything and start your own Hero's Journey. You will be amazed what you find on the way!

I choose to start my Hero's Journey on: (date)

(Details of Hero's Journey workshops are given at the back of the book.)

Step 7
Having fun and taking time out

Some people skip this final step in our programme and just keep on working. Others go to the other extreme and try to have fun all the time! Neither approach works. You have to take a middle path. You can't work all the time, or you will burn out. Equally, you cannot party all the time – you will kill yourself with overindulgence and boredom.

Interesting fact

The Irish international rugby and football teams all have one vital element in their training: a good dose of R&R ('rest and relaxation'). Detailed psychological and physiological research shows that R&R forms a vital part of getting fit. Without R&R, you would never perform well.

For an example of this, we will turn to soccer. In the 1990s, when Jack Charlton's Irish football team was beating the world, you could always get the autographs of the players the night before a vital World Cup match.

How? You would think they would be studying the opposition or going through tactics.

Not at all! The night before the big match, they would go out for the night to a well-known Dublin cinema, where they would relax in front of the latest Hollywood blockbuster. If you stood by the door after the show, the players would all troop out, relaxed and joking, and it would always be possible to get an autograph. Jack knew that his players needed rest and relaxation before the big occasion. Now all the top athletes in the world build R&R into their training schedules – and you should too. If you have R&R, you will perform better. If you don't, you will underperform.

Questionnaire: Am I getting enough rest, fun and relaxation in my life?

	Agree	Disagree
	10 9 8 7 6 5 4 3 2 1 0	

Statement	Score
Every day, I find time for myself, when I can relax and unwind	0
I find regular time to relax and have fun with my partner/children	5
When I am stressed out, I take a complete break and relax before returning to the fray	0
I find time to relax at weekends and I take regular holidays	6
I have a good laugh at least once a day	3
I have good friends who I can share a good laugh with	4
I have a good balance in my life between stress and taking time out	5
My family, friends and work colleagues would not describe me as an 'uptight' person and enjoy my company	7
I do not need alcohol, drugs or other artificial means to relax and have fun	6
I find I have an appetite for life – overall, I enjoy it!	8

44

161

100–80	You are having a lot of rest and fun in your life – well done! You will live a longer and healthier life as a result
79–70	You are happy enough but have some room for improvement
69–50	You are getting by but need to improve the balance between work, rest and relaxation in your life significantly
49–40	You are not enjoying life anywhere near as much as you could
39 and below	You are jeopardising your health and making yourself and your family unhappy. You need urgently to review the lack of fun and relaxation in your life

Taking time out: sharpening the saw

Q: If you were a lumberjack, cutting down trees in the forest, would you work non-stop all day with a blunt axe?

A: No, you would sharpen your axe first. If you did otherwise, you would suffer the problem of diminishing returns. For with a sharp axe, you will fell ten trees a day, while with a blunt axe you will only fell two, and as you get paid for the number of trees you fell and not the number of hours you work, you are going to lose out financially.

This is what is increasingly happening to workers who are driven by the Celtic Tiger. They are too fearful to stop and take a break, so they go on working until their performance is blunted. Poor efficiency and dangerous work practices result.

Fascinating facts

Q: What do the Three Mile Island nuclear accident and Chernobyl have in common?

A: The staff involved in monitoring the situations in both catastrophes were found to be suffering from exhaustion caused by lack of sleep. They were not able to take evasive action in time. As a result, hundreds of people died as a consequence of radiation and will continue to do so for generations.

Research worldwide shows that numerous man-made accidents are due to human error caused by overwork and lack of sleep. Most ship, train, plane and automobile accidents are partly a result of driver exhaustion. Not taking time out to sharpen your axe can lead to accidents and even death!

Do I take enough rest in the course of my daily and weekly schedule?

Check your weekly schedule:

What sort of sleep and rest breaks do I get on:

Monday
Tuesday
Wednesday
Thursday
Friday
Saturday
Sunday

How many holidays/weekend breaks do I take each year?

How can I increase the amount of rest I get?
(Tick the relevant boxes)

Get to bed earlier ☐
Have siesta breaks ☐
Have power snoozes ☐
Take weekends breaks ☐
Have holidays away ☐
Take up yoga, t'ai chi or exercise ☐
Book in regular massage sessions ☐
Other:

I have decided to increase my rest/relaxation sessions in the following ways:

1

2

3

I have decided to take ☐ (number of) holidays this year

Taking regular breaks helps your health - Not taking breaks causes health breakdown

Studies of top athletes have shown that overtraining leads to all sorts of problems, including:

How important is fun in your life?

- overuse injuries
- breakdown of the immune system
- recurring low-grade infections
- long-term damage to heart muscle

Not taking regular breaks from work is bad for your health. We all need to take regular breaks in order to allow our body and mind to renew themselves.

Taking time out lets you see the bigger picture

Have you heard the expressions 'She's so strung out she can't see the wood for the trees' or 'He can't get anything done – he's always chasing his tail'? When we become involved in a big project at work, or are caught up with a major decision at home, we can soon lose sight of our goals.

Take writing as an example. You can have an idea for a book or novel and begin writing, but eventually you run into a brick wall. It is then that you put the manuscript in a drawer and leave it for a month. When you come back, you see everything in a new light. The break has done you good: it has given you back perspective on the subject. You can start writing again.

Question: Are you too close to some problem in your life? Do you need a break?

Problem:

Solution: I will take a break. (Write down the time, place and duration of the break)

Time out allows you to wonder: Plato's prognosis

The Greek philosopher Plato was insistent that people should take out time to wonder about life and our place in it. 'A life without wonder is a useless life,' he once said.

Do you take time out just to wonder? Perhaps not. The Celtic Tiger is a cruel taskmaster, and taking time out to wonder about life would be seen as wasting time. 'Get up and get on with it!' your manager, partner or teacher roars! You can't waste time doing nothing! But are they right?

Fascinating fact: Doing nothing is good for your brain!

Behavioural scientists have discovered that our most productive time may well be the time we spend doing nothing. They discovered that those aimless moments spent wondering about town having coffee, gazing at the crowds passing by, meandering through a bookshop or sitting on a park bench looking at the ducks are all precious times when we 'incubate' ideas and make breakthroughs with personal problems.

It can also be the time when great discoveries are made, like Archimedes in his bath or Sir Isaac Newton lying under a tree on a summer's day 'thinking'!

Q: Are you taking time out to incubate your ideas or wonder about your place in the universe?

A: Yes ☐ No☐

If 'Yes', where and when?

If 'No', can I make time to wonder and incubate ideas?

When?
Where?

Tips on how to take more time out

If you find from the questionnaire on page 153 that you are not taking time out, here are a few tips:

- Organise yourself. Buy a small diary and each night set aside five minutes to prioritise and schedule in your next day
- Write a hit list of the things you have to do tomorrow – especially things that you have been putting off
- Then fill in the day schedule as shown below. (You can do all this on a scrap of paper as well as in the diary!)

Hit List
Phone bank manager about overdraft
Ring John and organise birthday celebration
Get Pat's money for phone bill
Pay solicitor's bill
Finish letter to Joan saying I will not be coming over for Christmas

Day Schedule
9 am	Pop into post office on way to work to post letter and pay phone bill
10 am	Work
11 am	Work
12 noon	Work
1 pm	Lunch: look for Sean's birthday gift and buy toothbrush and toothpaste

2 pm	Work
3 pm	Work
4 pm	Work
5 pm	Work
6 pm	Buy groceries in supermarket and coffee beans from Bewley's
7 pm	Get off bus two stops early and walk through park for last half a mile
8 pm	Dinner
9 pm	TV news
10 pm	Set up candles/scent and tape machine in bathroom and relax in bath for thirty minutes

Bed by 11.30 pm

The problem with hit lists and schedules is keeping to them, but if you do, you will be amazed at the results!

Having more fun in your life!

This should be the easy part of life but is often the hardest. I bump into many people who are so stressed out by family commitments and work that they resemble wrung-out dishcloths. If you asked them if they were having fun in their lives, they would throttle you while screaming, 'When do I have time for fun?'

But life without fun is not life – it's a chore. Fill in the questionnaire on fun again:

	Yes	No
I find regular time to have fun with my partner and/or children	☐	☐
I have a good laugh at least once a day	☐	☐
I have good friends who I can share a good laugh with	☐	☐
My family, friends and work colleagues would not describe me as an 'up-tight' person; they enjoy my company	☐	☐
I do not need alcohol, drugs or other artificial means to relax and have fun	☐	☐
I find I have an appetite for life – overall, I enjoy it!	☐	☐

If you gave three or more 'yes' answers, you are on the way to having a fun life. If you gave two 'Yes' answers or less, you definitely need more fun in your life.

Why do I need more fun in my life?

Fun is creative

Research shows that fun is an integral part of creativity. Some of the greatest ideas come when people are having fun. Computer companies like Apple and Microsoft, filmmaking organisations like Dreamworks, and producers of hit television shows such as *Friends* all realise the creativity released when people have fun and make their planning meetings as fun as possible. The reason is simple: fun allows for the absurd. It enables us to see life from unexpected angles.

Fun meetings have generated ideas that have changed the world. Steve Jobs, the creator of Apple Computers and the man chiefly responsible for the advent of the personal computer, is just such a man. He attributed his success to the atmosphere at Apple in the early days of the company, when the young college whizz-kids working for him were allowed to go wild at creative meetings, coming up with all sorts of wacky and wonderful ideas. These meetings were fun, and some of the suggestions went on to become products that would change the lives of everyone living on the planet.

Have fun and you will be more creative!

Fun recharges the batteries

Ever felt drained and exhausted? You are walking glumly down the street when you bump into an old friend and decide to go for a chat. Suddenly you are remembering old times and old friends, and the laughter comes. Soon you are belly-laughing as you recall the past and the crazy things you got up to. By the time you and your friend part, your eyes are filled with tears of laugher and all signs of fatigue are gone. You say goodbye and turn to leave, realising that you suddenly feel on top of the world.

Laughter is a great reviver – literally – for it fills you with more oxygen as you take in huge gulps of air while laughing. Laughter and fun revive your spirits and recharge your batteries like nothing else.

Fun makes you healthier

There is a famous case of an American cancer sufferer who, on hearing he had only weeks to live, went to his local video store and took out dozens of comedy films. For a week he did nothing but look at them and belly-laugh. In the end, he cured his cancer.

In a way, this is hardly surprising, for all the medical research shows that sad people (for example, those who have suffered the death of a close partner) are more prone to illness and sudden death than the rest of us. It seems that happiness makes us healthier. Studies show that happy people flood their bodies with certain chemicals when they laugh – chemicals that bolster the immune system and help us fight off illness and disease. Have a good laugh – it will make you healthier, and could save your life!

How to have more fun in your life

Here are some ideas on how to have more fun. They will require a bit of effort – but they will be worth it:

- Look up an old friend. Pick up the phone and talk. Arrange to meet for a drink or a chat. Memories always provide fun.
- Organise a party and invite friends, neighbours or work colleagues round. Put on some music, tell gags and interact.
- Get dressed up and go out on the town. Try one of the many comedy stores that have sprung up in local pubs and clubs. You cannot help but laugh at a good professional comedien.
- Or get out your favourite comedy video, get in a bottle of wine and a few beers, invite a few friends round and see what happens.
- While walking down the street, smile at someone who catches our eye. You will be surprised at the reaction.
- In all things, be proactive and take the initiative – live!

In conclusion:
A summary of the seven steps to a happier family

The seven steps are all about living more fully:

Step 1   Having a healthy body
Step 2   Having a healthy spirit
Step 3   Developing your emotional intelligence
Step 4   Enjoying a good sex life
Step 5   Enjoying healthy relationships
Step 6   Enjoying your work
Step 7   Enjoying time out and fun

The seven steps are not a quick fix. They require work and change – but if you go through the questionnaires and exercises and make even small changes, you will gain great benefit.

In the end, we all want a happy life, and those who choose to have families want a happy *family* life as well. On one level, this is not always possible. We do not experience happiness all the time, either in our own lives or in our family lives. Life is too unpredictable for that – too full of disappointments, sudden accidents, reversals and unexpected deaths. Life can be truly terrible – depending on your circumstances and where you live – and is sprinkled with tragedy.

But in the spaces between the tragedies are moments of grace and serendipity, where good fortune and coincidence help us lead happier lives. This is where our book comes in and you start to make decisions to improve your life through the seven steps.

In the space below, note the changes you are choosing to make (remember, you don't have to choose to make *any* changes) and the time when you are going to start to make those changes.

		Changes I will make	Start date
Step 1	Having a healthy body		
Step 2	Having a healthy spirit		
Step 3	Developing my emotional intelligence		
Step 4	Enjoying a good sex life		
Step 5	Enjoying healthy relationships		
Step 6	Enjoying work		
Step 7	Enjoying time out and fun		

Tips on making and sticking to decisions

Eating the elephant

If you were asked to eat an elephant, you would quail. It is far too enormous a task! In the end, the prospect of eating it would keep you from doing anything. It would terrify you.

The only way to eat an elephant would be to break it down into tiny, daily chunks. A bit of a foot here, a portion of ear there. By breaking the elephant down into digestible chunks in this way, you would eventually be able to eat the whole thing.

The same applies to making and keeping decisions: break the task (whatever it is) down into tiny portions and do a bit of it each day! That way, you will succeed. Sometimes the thing that defeats us is the enormity of the task facing us. Remember, break things down into digestible chunks – eat the elephant piece by piece and you will succeed!

We were going to call this book 7 Steps to a Happy Family. In the end, we called it 7 Steps to a Happier Family, because every step you take to improve yourself and live more fully will have a direct impact on your family. It is they who will gain from the improvements you make in your life, who will learn from the example you set and who will enjoy life more fully. You really can make your family happier – and it all starts by first changing yourself! Good luck on your journey: I know you'll make it!

Other books by
Kevin Flanagan

Maximum Points – Minimum Panic. Marino Books, 1996. This book was No. 1 in the paperback bestseller list in both 1996 and 1997.

Everyday Genius. Marino Books, 1997. In his foreword, Professor Eugene Gendlin of the University of Chicago described this as one of the best books ever written on the subject of focusing therapy and empathetic listening.

How to Get Your Child Maximum Points. Marino Books, 2000. The follow-up to the bestselling *Maximum Points – Minimum Panic.*

Rights outside Ireland for these three books are now available.

Kevin Flanagan gives workshops and talks, based on the books he has written, to schools, colleges and business and various adult groups. Kevin can be contacted at kevinflanagan@eircom.net or on (086) 606 2868. You can reach Brian Mooney at brianjmooney@hotmail.com or on (01) 288 8533.